MESOAMERICA'S
ANCIENT
CITIES

Frontispiece: The Castillo at Chichén Itzá from the Temple of the Warriors.

MESOAMERICA'S ANCIENT CITIES

AERIAL VIEWS
OF PRECOLUMBIAN RUINS
IN MEXICO, GUATEMALA, BELIZE,
AND HONDURAS

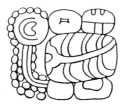

William M. Ferguson
and Arthur H. Rohn

Photographs by John Q. Royce
and William M. Ferguson

Foreword by R.E.W. Adams

University Press of Colorado
NIWOT, COLORADO

Emblem glyphs on title page, left to right: Quiriguá, Palenque, Copán.

Printing and binding by Toppan Printing Company (America), Inc.
Composition by Keystone Typesetting, Inc., Orwigsburg, Pennsylvania.
Design by Barbara Jellow.

Printed in Japan

Library of Congress Cataloging-in-Publication Data

Ferguson, William M.
  Mesoamerica's ancient cities : aerial views of precolumbian ruins in Mexico,
Guatemala, Belize, and Honduras / William M. Ferguson and Arthur H. Rohn ;
photographs by John Q. Royce and William M. Ferguson.
     p.   cm.
  Includes bibliographical references.
  ISBN 0-87081-173-8
  1. Indians of Mexico—Antiquities—Aerial photographs. 2. Indians of
Central America—Antiquities—Aerial photographs. 3. Mexico—Antiquities—
Aerial photographs. 4. Central America—Antiquities—Aerial photographs.
I. Rohn, Arthur H., 1929–   . II. Royce, John Q. III. Title.
F1219.F35   1990
917.2'0022'2—dc20   90-12175
                                                              CIP

First Edition

All Rights Reserved

The University Press of Colorado
is a cooperative publishing enterprise
supported, in part, by

Adams College,
Colorado State University,
Fort Lewis College,
Mesa State College,
Metropolitan State College,
University of Colorado,
University of Northern Colorado,
University of Southern Colorado,
and Western State College.

The paper used in this publication meets the minimum requirements of the
American National Standard for Information Sciences—Permanence of Paper
for Printed Library Materials.
ANSI Z39.48–1984

Contents

Illustrations

Foreword

Amateurs have justly earned and enjoyed a good reputation in Maya archaeology and in other disciplines of Mesoamerican study. Many of them have made lasting and notable contributions to the field and in the end they became true professionals. John Lloyd Stephens and Frederick Catherwood, founders of Maya studies, were only the first of a number of distinguished investigators whose initial interests and efforts were in other areas (the law and architecture in their cases). Alfred Maudslay, who left a budding career in the foreign service of the British Empire, and Teobert Maler, who (somewhat less voluntarily) left the military service of Maximilian and Carlota, devoted the rest of their lives to the study of Maya ruins. More recently, the field has benefited immensely by the fact that, during the Depression, Tatiana Proskouriakoff could not find a job in architecture. She eventually made fundamental contributions to our understanding of the architecture, art, and, above all, the writing of the Maya. Now William Ferguson and John Royce add their names to the list of intellectual benefactors. I hasten to add that their colleague, Arthur Rohn, is a professional's professional although specialized in another area of the New World. However, he also brings a new perspective to the Mesoamerican field from his prior and different experience.

This book is another in the notable series that this trio has produced on archaeological subjects seen literally from a new perspective—that is, from the air. Maya ruins are particularly intractable to aerial photography with a few exceptions. Other aspects of Mesoamerica lend themselves more easily to aerial photography. However, it is one thing to take a photograph and another to achieve an informed and aesthetically pleasing view. The considerable persistence and skill shown in the aerial photos contained in this book are therefore even more remarkable, considering the handicaps under which they were made. The supplementary photographs are equally excellent in my judgment and allow one to advance from a distant view to a detailed examination, which is very difficult and even painful on site. For this reason alone the book would be worth owning.

However, and additionally, the text is impressively free of the "gee-whiz" atmosphere and the pretentiousness that often characterize writing about Mesoamerican archaeology for the general public. The latest material is carefully presented in a lively style, but the authors have avoided overwhelming detail. One of the interesting possibilities of a book of this kind is that one can lure scholars to say things that are stimulating and daring and that they would usually not advance for a professional audience. Often these ideas, covered with appropriate (and unfortunately, stuffy) language, may eventually appear as the guides to research for the next generation. Perhaps Ferguson and Royce's persuasive skills developed from their law and political professions.

Finally, one of the most attractive things about this book and the others that Ferguson, Royce, and Rohn have produced, is that they obviously have had fun doing them. As a result, this book is also fun to read and reflects the fact that most archaeologists genuinely enjoy what they do. No humorless essays into hypothetico-deductive systems here; nor are they necessary. The reader will find a solid but enjoyable introduction to Mesoamerican civilizations as well as information about specific ruins. Once again amateurs (although they have now probably lost that status) have made a genuine contribution to the field.

Richard E. W. Adams

Preface

The mountains and jungles of southern Mexico and northern Central America no longer house "lost cities" or "mysterious forgotten empires." During recent decades scholars have taken the mystery out of the ancient cultures of Mesoamerica. The names of the kings of Palenque and Tikal, for instance, are now almost as well known as the emperors of Rome. In this book we have described and photographed more than fifty ancient cities.

"Meso(middle)america" describes a cultural region that extended in Precolumbian times from north of the Valley of Mexico (now the site of the world's largest city, Ciudad de Mexico), southeastward to Honduras in Central America. The nearly 800 miles (by air) from the ruins of Tula on the north edge of the Valley of Mexico to ancient Copán in northwest Honduras includes southeast Mexico, the Yucatán Peninsula, Belize, Guatemala, and a portion of Honduras. Within the boundaries of Mesoamerica are the mountains of southern Mexico and Guatemala, the swamps of Mexico's southern Gulf Coast, the low flat hardlands of Yucatán, and the rain forests of the Petén in the Guatemala lowlands. Each of these regions was the home of a brilliant Prehispanic civilization.

Spanning three thousand years between 1500 B.C. and A.D. 1500, great Indian civilizations flourished, waned, and died: Olmec, Teotihuacán, Maya, Toltec, Zapotec, and others. The Aztec and other Indian cultures viable in the A.D. 1500s were destroyed by the Spanish *conquistadores*. Western cultures such as Minoan, Greek, Carthagenian, Roman, Venetian, and Byzantine both exhibited the same general characteristics of civilization and rose and fell during the same span of years.

The civilized Mesoamericans left for posterity the ruins of their cities. We have flown above, walked over, and climbed around these ruins to take photographs for this book. At ground level, ancient ruins often appear to be no more than piles of rocks, but from the air those rubble mounds and masonry walls become buildings and cities. We have included 51 such sites shown in 81 aerial photographs, many accompanied by schematic drawings to identify standing structures. Of the 353 illustrations, 259 are in color. The aerial photographs were taken during flights to Mexico and Central America made in preparation for two previous books, *Maya Ruins of Mexico in Color* and *Maya Ruins in Central America in Color*. We have included ground photographs of most sites to show the intriguing aspects of each ruin and to demonstrate the diversity of Mesoamerican art and architecture during Preclassic, Classic, and Postclassic times. All the included ruins are sufficiently excavated and restored to make a visit interesting and rewarding.

Within the past twenty years, linguists, epigraphers, art historians, ethnologists, and archaeologists have combined their talents to decipher the Maya glyphic writing, reconstruct the settlement patterns, demonstrate the existence of intensive agriculture, widespread trade, and city states, and bring to life these people of the past—how they were governed, the gods they worshiped, and the way they lived.

We have recently revisited many of the sites to photograph the results of continued excavation and restoration and to insure that the text includes current research.

We have rather arbitrarily divided *Mesoamerica's Ancient Cities* into nine regions: Central Mexico, Valley of Oaxaca, Lowland Maya, Belize, Chiapas, Guatemala Highlands, Río Bec, Puuc, and Northern Yucatán. The introduction encapsulates Mesoamerican culture from the early nomads to the arrival of Cortez—from 2500 B.C. to A.D. 1520.

These are some of the most spectacular of Mesoamerican ruins. The great city of Teotihuacán in the Valley of Mexico may have grown to 200,000 people during the time it dominated Mesoamerica, between A.D. 450 and 650. The Aztecs nearly 1,000 years later viewed the city's ruins with awe. To the northwest of Teotihuacán (several hundred years after its fall), the Toltecs built Tula and later conquered Yucatán and rebuilt Chichén Itzá. Before Teotihuacán existed, the Olmecs had moved into the Mexican highlands and established Chalcatzingo, a city south of modern Puebla. Not far from Cuernavaca, Xochicalco, with its striking Temple displaying Maya connections, began to flourish in late Classic times—around A.D. 700.

In the Valley of Oaxaca, ruins surrounding the city of Oaxaca evidence occupation for at least 3,000 years before the discovery of America. Zapotec Monte Albán, now excavated and partially restored, was one of the first city-states. These people, without a beast of burden, metal tools, or the wheel, leveled a mountain top entirely by hand and erected a timeless series of masonry buildings and pyramids. Down the Pan-American Highway to the southeast of Oaxaca sits Mitla of the Mixtecs; its buildings exhibit Mesoamerica's most incredible mosaic stonework.

The Maya were the most advanced of all the Precolumbian cultures in the New World; they were master builders, astronomers, and mathematicians, and, above all, they had a fully developed written language. In the lowland Guatemala jungles the temple pyramids of Tikal rise above the tropical rain forest of the Petén. Active excavation and restoration of Tikal have been going on for thirty years, making the ruins of this Classic Maya city one of the wonders of Mesoamerica. Now that the Maya glyphs can be translated, Tikal's tombs and stelae tell us the names of its kings and much of its history. At Quiriguá, a beautiful ruin nestled in an ocean of green

banana trees, great stelae, the largest in Mayaland, were carved and set up for the aggrandisement of Cauac Sky. One stela relates the capture and execution of 18 Rabbit, king of Copán.

Copán, often referred to as the Athens of the Maya, has been the subject of intensive study. Its Hieroglyphic Stairway, made up of some 2,500 glyph blocks—the largest known Maya glyph panel—is being restored and the blocks are being placed in proper sequence. The lineages of its kings are being revealed.

The ruins in the Guatemala highlands scattered along the Continental Divide between Guatemala City and Mexico were fortified Postclassic Maya cities: Utatlán, Iximché, Mixco Viejo, and Zaculeu. These cities were conquered and sacked by the invading Spaniards in the early 1500s. Xunantunich on the Belize-Guatemala border displays a monumental, restored frieze that extends across one entire side of the Castillo. At recently discovered Kohunlich located west of Chetumal, Mexico, large human-like Sun God masks flank the west-facing staircase of a temple-pyramid.

Palenque's restored ruins, located in a tropical park, are beautifully situated on the face of a forest-covered mountain. Deep inside the Temple of the Inscriptions, accessible by the original hidden stairway, lies the famous crypt and sepulchre of Lord Shield Pacal, the great king of Palenque who ruled during the A.D. 600s.

In Yucatán, three of the best known and frequently visited ruins are Uxmal, Chichén Itzá, and Tulum. Both Uxmal and Chichén Itzá are well-supported with tourist accommodations. Uxmal is not only a spectacular late Classic Maya site, it is the key to four additional Puuc ruins now accessible by a new paved highway: Kabah, Sayil, Xlapak, and Labná. The architecture of Chichén Itzá displays the transition from the Maya Classic Puuc to Toltec (Mexican) style. Tulum, a little Postclassic frontier trading town, was still inhabited when first seen by the Spaniards in 1518.

Mesoamerica's Ancient Cities has been a labor of love—the result of years of flying, photography, travel, and research. We hope we have produced a view of the magnificent Precolumbian ruins that will please interested and intelligent readers.

William M. Ferguson
Arthur H. Rohn
John Q. Royce

Introduction

Meso(middle)america is the name given to the region south of a line crossing central Mexico beginning at Tampico on the Gulf of Mexico and extending to Mazatlán on the Gulf of California, and north of a line crossing Honduras beginning at San Pedro Sula to the Golfo de Fonseca on the Pacific Ocean. This area encompasses modern-day central and southern Mexico, Belize, Guatemala, and western Honduras. In this book we will explore the ancient cultural regions of Mesoamerica: Valley of Mexico, Valley of Oaxaca, Gulf Coast of Mexico, the Yucatán Peninsula, Chiapas, the highlands of Guatemala, and the Maya lowlands of Guatemala, Belize, and western Honduras.

Mesoamerica's distinctive cultural features, which developed prior to the arrival of the Spaniards in the early A.D. 1500s, include a sophisticated calendar; a base-20 numerical system utilizing the concept of zero; hieroglyphic writing; codices or books; maps; an advanced knowledge of astronomy; ritual ballgames; crop staples of maize, beans, chilies, and squash; organized markets using cacao beans for money; distinctive artistic and architectural styles; sacrificial bloodletting; wars of conquest; and wars engaged to capture sacrificial victims.

EARLY MAN IN MESOAMERICA

An Asian branch of mankind crossed the land bridge from Siberia to Alaska during the last Ice Age, which had lowered the oceans making what is now the Bering Sea into a broad grass-covered highway between the continents. These people were ancestral American Indians. Archaeologists suggest various dates for the beginning of the migrations. The most conservative suggests a date around 11,000 B.C., M. D. Coe feels people were living in the Valley of Mexico as early as 24,000 years ago. William Irving's find of fossil bone tools along the Yukon River in Alaska suggests an era between 26,000 to 29,000 years ago; and R.E.W. Adams suggests there is some evidence that man arrived in the Western Hemisphere as early as 35,000 years ago. As the migrant Indians filtered throughout North, Central, and South America, many groups settled in various parts of the Western Hemisphere and developed individual characteristics and traditions.

Richard S. MacNeish's work in the Tehuacán Valley near Puebla, Mexico, disclosed a late Pleistocene occupation by nomadic hunter-gatherers prior to 7000 B.C. These people lived on animals they could kill, from huge mammoths to small game. Some plants were domesticated by 7000 B.C. and sometime between 5000 and 3400 B.C. they began raising small amounts of corn, avocados, chili peppers, amaranth, squash, and beans. MacNeish and others working in the Maya lowlands in Belize have found evidence of ancient hunter-gatherer Indians who lived there from about 9000 to 7500 B.C. and of fishing peoples who lived along the coast of Belize about 4000 B.C. Norman Hammond's excavations at Cuello in north-central Belize indicate the earliest known Maya agricultural villages (about 2500 B.C.), followed by continuous occupation to the Classic Maya period. Hammond concludes that the Maya were mainstream Mesoamericans with as long a prehistory as the inhabitants of Oaxaca or the Valley of Mexico and that their late Preclassic society was not the result of cultural stimulus or population movement from other parts of Mesoamerica. All of the Mesoamerican Classic cultures seem to have grown out of locally indigenous early populations.

The change from hunting and gathering to food production in Mesoamerica took place very gradually over many thousands of years. The Indians began to settle down as their success at domesticating wild plants (like chili and maize) improved. Chilies and some squashes, the first plants to be domesticated in Mexico (around 7000 B.C.), were followed by pumpkins, beans, and maize. With corn came manos and metates, wattle-and-daub houses by 2500 B.C., and then pottery by around 1500 B.C. However, the impact of agriculture on society did not really take effect until close to 2500 B.C. when people started living in villages and depended on what they raised, supplemented by some hunting and collecting.

MESOAMERICAN CIVILIZATION

By 1500 to 1000 B.C., we find the foundations of Mesoamerican civilization beginning to appear—focal ceremonial centers, intensive irrigation agriculture, a stratified social system with elite rulers, evidence of a calendar, and monumental stonework.

The term "Classic" was originally applied to the cultures of ancient Greece and Rome, particularly to the periods when the best literature, art, architecture, and other fine arts were produced. In Mesoamerica, "Classic" refers to a florescence of civilization roughly between A.D. 150 and 900. "Preclassic" refers to the cultural stage before the Classic and "Postclassic" to the times following. As we learn more about Mesoamerican civilizations, it becomes apparent that more advances were made in Preclassic times than previously thought and that the Postclassic was not a time of cultural decadence.

Mesoamerican Chronology

Preclassic (formative)

Early	2500–1000 B.C.	
Middle	1000–300 B.C.	
Late	300 B.C.–A.D. 150 to 300	

Classic

Early	A.D. 150 to 300–600	
Late	A.D. 600–900	

Postclassic

Early	A.D. 900–1200	
Late	A.D. 1200–1520	

Preclassic Preclassic culture provided the background for Mesoamerican civilized life, which was fostered by the arts and technology of the early Olmecs, Maya, Zapotecs, and peoples in the Valley of Mexico. At the same time the Olmec civilization was developing along the coast of the Gulf of Mexico, villages were beginning to evolve in central Mexico along the shores of Lake Texcoco (now covered by Mexico City), and the Maya culture began stirring in central and northern Belize, the Yucatán, and in the lowlands of northern Guatemala.

A distinctive Maya culture developed by around 1200 B.C., according to Norman Hammond: "the Maya were not the poor cousins of the Olmec and the highland peoples, but the authors of their own cultural history, creators rather than merely borrowers" (Hammond 1986:400).

By 300 B.C. the Maya were living in more or less organized societies from Yucatán to Honduras. Centers of population became more numerous and the largest villages evolved into cities with plazas lined by pyramids and temples. During the late Preclassic, in the Guatemala highlands at Kaminaljuyú, the opulence of the nobles suggests that they held great economic and political power. The numerous massive buildings and fine burials indicate a fully developed and stratified society. Vibrant intellectual life, as well as economic and social organization, existed during the late Preclassic: buildings at Uaxactún (Structure E-VII Sub), Cerros, Tikal, and El Mirador were decorated with monumental sculpture. The self-aggrandizement of kings on stone stelae began.

The Preclassic Zapotecs of the Valley of Oaxaca used the bar-and-dot numbering system, the 260-day Almanac Year, the 52-year cycle, the Calendar Round, and hieroglyphic inscriptions. During this time they built palaces and temples. During the Preclassic, both the Olmec and Zapotec peoples developed the beginnings of a written language. Preclassic times set the stage for burgeoning cities and regional states over most of Mesoamerica.

For many years archaeologists and historians disagreed over where the Olmecs, the makers of huge basalt heads wearing semblances of old-fashioned football helmets, fit into Precolumbian Mesoamerican chronology. Some placed the Olmecs at around A.D. 800. Matthew Stirling, who did the original work at San Lorenzo, La Venta, and Tres Zapotes, argued the Olmecs created America's oldest civilization. The inscribed monuments and radiocarbon dates have shown he was correct. The Olmec site of San Lorenzo (on the Coatzacoalcos River southwest of Minatitlán, Mexico) flourished from 1200 to 900 B.C. When it was violently destroyed, La Venta on the Tonalá River to the east became the center of Olmec culture from 900 to 400 B.C.

CHRONOLOGIES

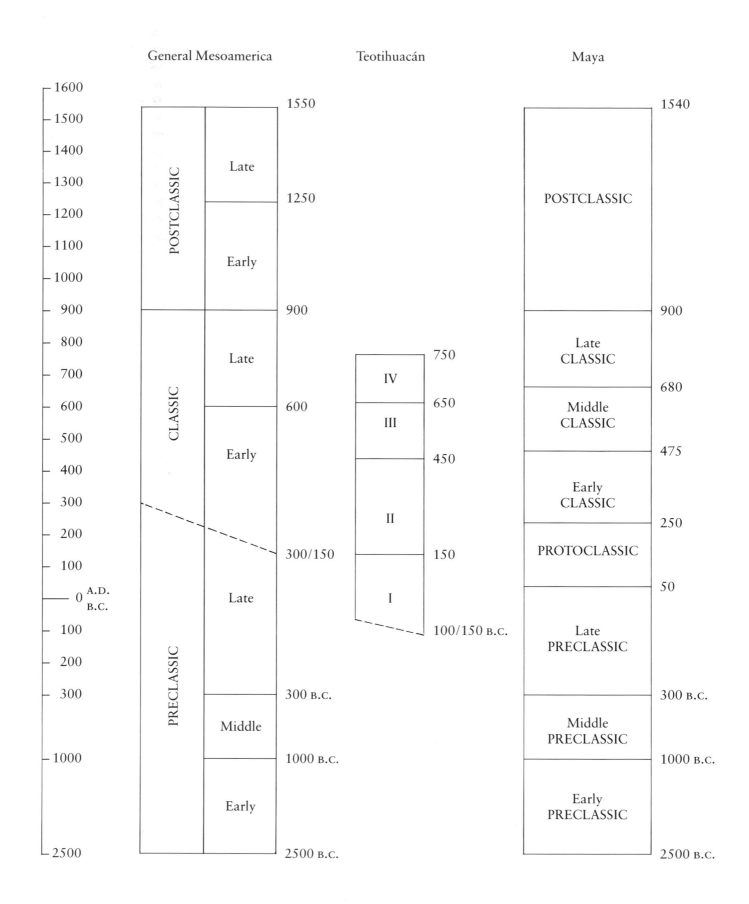

General Mesoamerica

Teotihuacán

Maya

1600		
1500	1550	1540
1400		
1300	Late	POSTCLASSIC
1200	1250	
1100	Early	
1000		
900	900	900
800		Late CLASSIC
700	Late	
600	600	680
500	Early	Middle CLASSIC
400		475
300		Early CLASSIC
200	300/150	
100		250
0 A.D. B.C.	Late	PROTOCLASSIC
100	100/150 B.C.	50
200		Late PRECLASSIC
300	300 B.C.	300 B.C.
1000	Middle	Middle PRECLASSIC
	1000 B.C.	1000 B.C.
	Early	Early PRECLASSIC
2500	2500 B.C.	2500 B.C.

POSTCLASSIC · CLASSIC · PRECLASSIC

Teotihuacán phases:
- IV — 750 / 650
- III — 650 / 450
- II — 450 / 150
- I — 150 / 100/150 B.C.

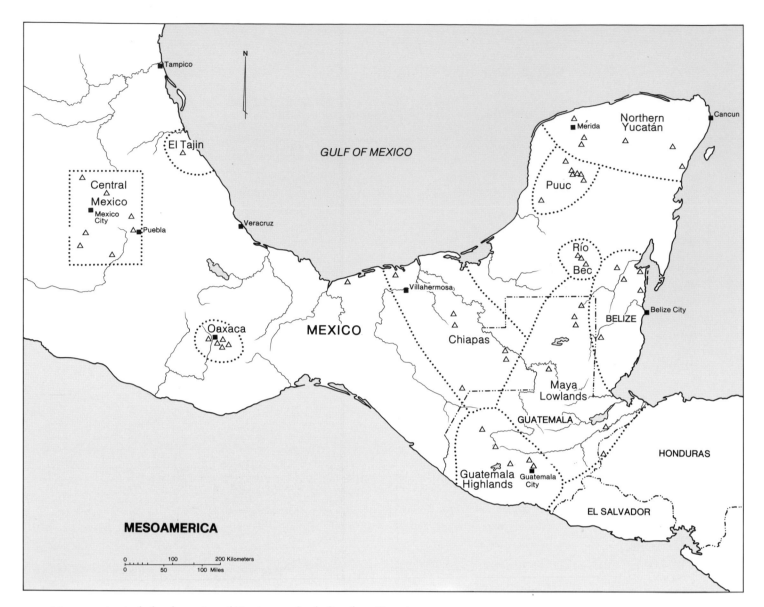

MESOAMERICA

Mesoamerica includes the region of Mexico south of a line from Tampico to Mazatlán, all of Guatemala, Belize, and the northwest corner of Honduras. The locations of Mesoamerica's ancient cities are designated by the symbol △. Each site is identified on the map included in each section.

Above: The ruins of La Venta of the ancient Olmecs now lie adjacent to an airstrip in Mexico's oil-producing region southeast of Vera Cruz. The green-covered mound is a conical-shaped pyramid more than 100 feet high that was constructed between 900 and 400 B.C. Below: Reconstruction drawing of the pyramid and ceremonial mounds at La Venta (After M.D. Coe).

The Olmec heartland—only about 50 miles wide—extended in an arc for about 125 miles along the southern shore of the Gulf of Mexico. In Olmec times, as now, it was a swampy land of high rainfall, forests, and savannahs, interlaced with rivers. Today it is part of Mexico's southern oil patch.

Unlike the Maya Indians whose descendants still live with us, nothing is known about the people who built the Olmec civilization other than the traces they left carved in stone and jade. The Olmecs are most famous for the colossal statues of heads—depicting their rulers—with thick lips and broad flat noses. Anthropologists report that there are still people living in southern Vera Cruz with thick lips and flat noses unlike the features of most Indians, but there is no traceable connection between them and the ancient Olmecs. Another feature of Olmec art is the were-jaguar, a cross between a jaguar and a human that is often represented as a baby with a snarling, feline mouth and cleft head.

Evidence of the Olmec culture also appears in the Valley of Oaxaca and in the Mexican highlands. Chalcatzingo, in the Amatzinac Valley about 40 miles southeast of Cuernavaca, is an important Olmec site consisting of platform mounds and terraces at the foot of one of three 1,000-foot peaks. Chalcatzingo was occupied from about 1500 B.C. to 500 B.C. The carvings on the rocks above the settlement in pure Olmec style were done between 700 and 500 B.C. while La Venta was flourishing.

In June 1984, the National Museum of Anthropology and History in Mexico City announced the discovery of an Olmec city located near the small town of Copalillo in Guerrero, about 100 miles south of Cuernavaca at the confluence of the Amacuzac and Balsas rivers. The site, named Teopantecuanitlan, is being excavated under the direction of Guadelupe Martinez Donjuan. To date his work has revealed two ballcourts, a stone-lined aqueduct, and large-scale stone architecture—a pyramid tentatively dated by radiocarbon methods to 1400 B.C. Sculptured were-jaguar faces and T-shaped monoliths with markings on the backs that might be bar-and-dot numerals have been discovered. If the bars and dots are numerals, they would be the oldest known. The site covers some 36 square miles and evidences three phases of occupation: (1) 1400 to 1200 B.C.—clay walls in the ceremonial center with carved clay masks; (2) 1200 to 800 B.C.—fitted stone walls and aqueducts, stone drains, and an interior court; and (3) 800 to 60 B.C.—six structures built in a semicircle plus a stone head. Some of the reliefs are similar in style to those at Chalcatzingo, some 60 miles to the northeast. This discovery of an Olmec ceremonial center, Teopantecuanitlan, in the mountains of central Mexico, will change many of the concepts now held about Mesoamerica's first civilization.

The legacy of the Olmec includes (1) recognition of an elite ruling class, (2) the aggrandizement of their rulers by the incredible effort involved in moving and carving the colossal heads and other stone monuments, (3) planned ceremonial centers, (4) monumental architecture, (5) elaborate headdresses, (6) ceremonial bars as status symbols, (7) ritual ball games, (8) bar-and-dot numeration, (9) capture and humiliation of prisoners, and (10) autosacrificial bloodletting ceremony practiced by the ruling class.

At La Venta the Olmecs built a volcano-shaped pyramid with petal-like sides about 100 feet high at the south end of a series of mounds creating a rectangular court. This very early ceremonial center, predating Teotihuacán and the Maya Classic centers by 1,000 years, must have been impressive, with multicolored clays used in the floors and platforms painted red, yellow, and purple. With the Olmec began Mesoamerica's great heritage of stone architecture.

Classic Archaeologists have arbitrarily divided the Classic period into early Classic (A.D. 150 to 600) and late Classic (A.D. 600 to 900). (Most of the photographs in this volume show restored Classic ruins.)

Soon after its construction, this La Venta abstract jaguar mask of serpentine blocks was covered with a layer of clay and a thick platform of bricks. It may now be seen at the La Venta Park in Villahermosa.

Above left: Olmec Monument 77 at La Venta Park represents a caped figure with a typical were-jaguar snarling mouth. Above: Typical of the Olmec culture were the flat-topped basalt blocks referred to as altars, which were actually thrones. Some weighed 40 tons. This one is Altar 4 at La Venta Park and displays a figure emerging from the open mouth of a jaguar. Left: Colossal heads with headgear resembling 1930s football helmets are a hallmark of the Olmec civilization (1200–400 B.C.). They are made of basalt, are 5 to 6 feet in height, and weigh many tons; each usually displays the individual insignia of the ruler.

Altar 5 at La Venta Park. A figure emerges from a niche holding an Olmec were-jaguar baby in his arms. On the side of the altar, adults are shown holding wriggling were-jaguar babies with characteristic turned-down mouths and cleft heads.

Much of this Golden Age in the New World occurred simultaneously with the Dark Ages in Europe. Beginning slightly before the reign of Constantine, Rome's first Christian emperor (A.D. 313), the Classic period coincided with the fall of the Roman Empire, the dominance of the Western world by the Byzantine Empire at Constantinople, and the birth of Mohammed (570) followed by the rise of Islam.

Three shining stars of the Early Classic were Teotihuacán in the Valley of Mexico, Monte Albán in the Valley of Oaxaca, and Tikal in the Petén of lowland Guatemala. At Maya Tikal the Classic begins shortly before A.D. 250 judging from Stela 29 dated A.D. 292.

One of the great kings of antiquity, the Maya king Stormy Sky, reigned during the 400s. Teotihuacán blossomed with new building and extended its influence over all of Mesoamerica to become one of the true cities of the world prior to its decline and destruction about A.D. 750. Since the Teotihuacán people had no writing—at least none has been preserved on their murals or ceramics—we know very little about who they were and certainly nothing about their rulers. At Monte Albán the Zapotecan-speaking people leveled a mountaintop on which they built huge stone buildings. By the end of the early Classic, the entire Valley of Oaxaca was dotted with settlements under the control of Monte Albán.

From A.D. 600 to 900, during the late Classic stage, Mesoamerican civilization flourished. Concurrently in the Old World, the Moslems conquered North Africa and moved into Spain. Charles Martel stopped their invasion of western Europe at the battles of Tours and Poitiers in A.D. 732. Over the next century, Charlemagne and the Franks ruled central Europe. In Mesoamerica, Maya Tikal reached its zenith under Ah Cacaw, whose rule began in A.D. 682. Other great Maya centers also flourished: Copán, Quiriguá, Palenque, and Yaxchilán, where hereditary kings and nobles intermarried and lived in great luxury. The Puuc sites around Uxmal in Yucatán were being constructed. The Maya, who were builders, astronomers, and writers, had a calendar at least as accurate as ours. Teotihuacán faltered and died, but in its place cities such as Cholula, Xochicalco, El Tajín, and Cacaxtla arose. In the Valley of Oaxaca, Monte Albán was largely abandoned. By A.D. 900 the Mesoamerican Classic came to an end.

Mesoamerica's Classic cultures were interrelated through trade, shared deities and ceremonies, military excursions, a common calendar and numeration systems, and art styles. The thrust of Teotihuacán south to Kaminaljuyú and Tikal and the influence of the Maya at Xochicalco and Cacaxtla represent this cross-fertilization. Central marketplaces and the network of trade routes by land and sea over all of Mesoamerica are evidence of the widespread commerce between cities and smaller regional centers. Cacao beans provided a medium of exchange. The ability of the Mesoamericans to produce and distribute goods through this marketing system was unsurpassed anywhere in the world.

Although Classic culture had virtually ended in the Maya southland by 800, it continued to flourish in the Yucatán and Puuc regions until nearly 1000. The Classic demise in the Petén was hastened by Maya raiders from the north who destroyed or conquered southern cities.

The rise of the north and the fall of the south was caused in part by a major shift in trade routes. The Chontal (or Putun Itzá) Maya, who lived on the south coast of the Gulf of Mexico in the vicinity of the modern city of Ciudad del Carmen, controlled the sea trade around the coast of Yucatán in late Classic times. These people traded with both the Maya of Yucatán and the Puuc and the Culhua-Mexica *pochteca* merchants of central Mexico. The Chontal Maya are believed to have cut off the major trade routes of the southern Maya and thus benefited (by their commerce) the cities of Yucatán and the Puuc: Uxmal, Dzibilchaltún, Chichén Itzá, and others. The trade to the west went to El Tajín, Cacaxtla, Xochicalco, and Toltec Tula (after A.D. 850) in the Mexican highlands. Jeff Kowalski suggests that the influence of these Chontal traders helps explain the "Mexican" features of the Puuc art and architecture in the 800s and early 900s. In the 900s, the Chontal along with the Toltecs of Tula moved into and took control of Yucatán.

Seibal, a Maya site located near the Pasión River about 40 miles southwest of Flores, Guatemala, shows evidence of the northern intrusion. This small center had a long history, beginning in the Preclassic, coeval with its neighbor Tikal. Only two of its structures have been restored.

The stelae erected early in Baktun 10 (after A.D. 830) show costume details and Tlaloc masks in central Mexican style. Stela 1 (A.D. 869) depicts a ruler who does not look Mayan—his nose is not rounded and his forehead is not slanted back—yet he wears Maya clothing and the inscription on the stela is Maya. On later stelae, the dates and inscriptions change to the Mexican style. Archaeologists disagree about the origin of these rulers. Mary Ellen Miller suggests the strong central Mexican influence indicates that the rulers of Seibal were Mexicanized Mayas, possibly the Olmeca-Xicalanca of the Gulf Coast. R.E.W. Adams is nearly certain that the elite rulers came from the Puuc where, after A.D. 800, the Maya show the Mexican influence.

Postclassic Mesoamerican civilization did not end with the Classic, but it changed. In the Maya regions, the Classic centers in lowland Guatemala, Belize, Honduras, and Chiapas, Mexico (among them Tikal, Quiriguá, Copán, Palenque, Yaxchilán, and Río Bec) were abandoned between A.D. 800 and 900. The Puuc Maya of Yucatán persisted into early Postclassic times, however.

Archaeologists have divided the Postclassic into early Postclassic (A.D. 900–1250) and late Postclassic (A.D. 1250–1550). In Mayaland, the Yucatan Peninsula and the Guatemala highlands became the primary centers of Postclassic culture. Chichén Itzá was conquered by the Chontal Maya from the Gulf Coast and by the Toltecs from the Mexican highlands. Northern Yucatán became a region of Mexicanized Maya urban centers where the military played a significant role in government. In Yucatán the Mexican influence was gradually overridden by Maya customs and traditions, and the strong centers of authority gave way to small independent chiefdoms. In the Guatemala highlands fortified centers, governed largely by a Mexican elite, sprang up. Today the Quiche Maya still live in the Guatemala highlands, and a large population of Yucatec Maya occupy Yucatán.

As we have seen, Monte Albán was abandoned as a residential site and Teotihuacán had been destroyed before the onset of the Postclassic. Early in the Postclassic, the Zapotecs founded the beautiful little center of Mitla in the Valley of Oaxaca. By A.D. 1350 Mixtec rulers had replaced the Zapotec chiefs throughout nearly the entire Oaxaca Valley.

Below: Pyramid A-III at Seibal lies about 40 miles south of Flores, Guatemala. Stelae adjacent to this temple evidence Toltec-Mexican influence, indicating that at the time they were erected—the early A.D. 800s, near the end of the Classic—the lowland Maya were being encroached upon by people from central Mexico. Left: The features of the figure on Stela 14 at Seibal indicate the ruler depicted was non-Maya and probably a Puuc region Mexican. (Photograph by Jerry Kelly).

Left: Stela 19 at Seibal combines Classic Maya and Mexican motifs. A speech sign (a Mexican symbol) comes from the lord's lips. At the same time he is performing the scattering gesture, probably representing the Classic Maya bloodletting ceremony. (Photograph by Jerry Kelly). Right: On the late Classic Stela 10 at Seibal, a lord with non-Maya features is shown with rather typical Classic Maya regalia. (Photograph by Jerry Kelly).

All Mesoamerica came under the influence of militarism, the glorification of war, and human sacrifice. Cities were fortified. Tula (ancient Tollan) of the Toltecs epitomized this sanguinary philosophy of the Postclassic with its devotion to the fierce god Tezcatlipoca (Smoking Mirror). For a while Tula was the seat of a mighty empire, but by the middle 1100s it too was abandoned by its factionalized inhabitants, most of whom moved into the Valley of Mexico. The power vacuum created by the fall of Tula resulted in the rise of independent city-states all over the Mexican highlands.

In the Valley of Mexico the Tepanecs, with the aid of upstart wanderers, the Aztecs, conquered all the city-states in the valley during the middle years of the 1300s. By 1426 the Aztecs defeated the Tepanecs and became the great power of Mexico. They assumed and claimed for themselves the accumulated heritage, culture, statecraft, and empire-building of the Toltecs. By the time of the Spanish conquest in the 1500s, as a result of their superior trade position and military power, the Aztecs came to dominate most of Mesoamerica, requiring subservience and tribute from millions of people. The Aztec belief that their gods needed the hearts of enemy warriors resulted in constant pillaging of other tribes for sacrificial victims—in 1487 some 20,000 captives were sacrificed for the dedication of the Great Temple at Tenochtitlán.

THE SPANISH CONQUEST

The arrogance and avarice of the Aztecs made them ripe for overthrow by their Indian enemies led by Cortez and a handful of Spanish soldiers in the early 1500s.

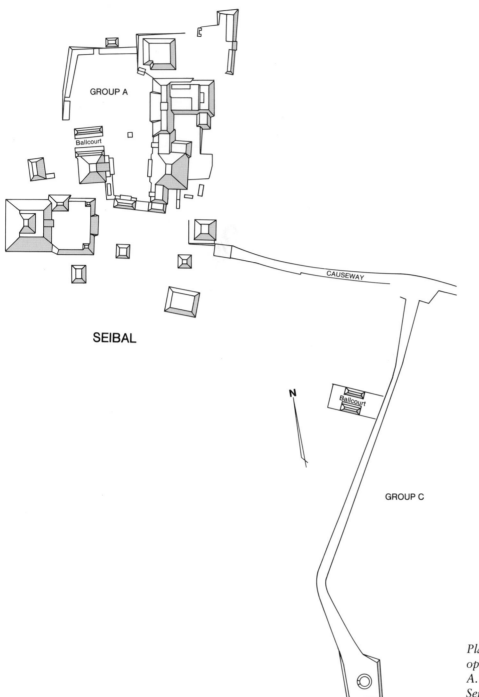

GROUP A

Ballcourt

SEIBAL

CAUSEWAY

N

Ballcourt

GROUP C

Plan of Seibal. Pyramid A-III sits in the open plaza in the south portion of Group A. The plan demonstrates the size of the Seibal core area.

Motecuhzoma Xocoyotzin (Montezuma), king of the Aztecs, was convinced that Cortez was the god Quetzalcoatl returning in 1519 according to an ancient Toltec prophesy. This incredible coincidence enabled the Spaniards to march unopposed into the Aztec capital of Tenochtitlán and take Montezuma prisoner. This event, plus the amazing fighting spirit of the Spaniards with their horses and cannon and the enthusiastic support of the Aztec enemies, enabled the Spaniards to destroy the Aztec empire.

Following the fall of Aztec Tenochtitlán, the Spaniards extended their power over all of Mexico and Central and South America. The Spaniards dedicated themselves to the destruction of Mesoamerican civilization because they considered it to be heathen. The Catholic church began a systematic and thorough program to convert the Indians. In doing so, the Church mingled the Precolumbian deities into the Catholic hierarchy of saints and assigned Christian names to the old deities. As a result, a distinctive Latin culture has grown up in Mexico and Central America. In western Guatemala, for example, Indians today believe that events in the life of Christ and many Biblical occurrences took place in Guatemala.

TEOPANZOLCO

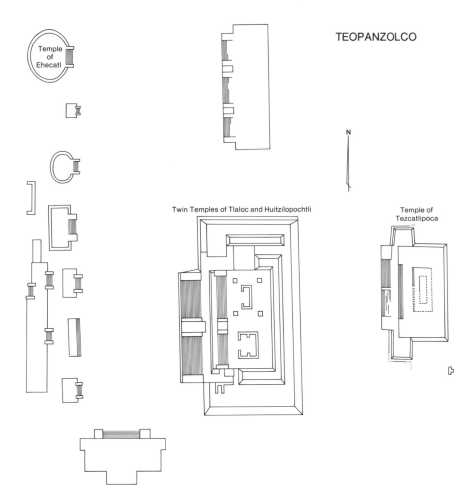

Temple of Ehecatl

Twin Temples of Tlaloc and Huitzilopochtli

Temple of Tezcatlipoca

N

Below: Teopanzolco, in northeast Cuernavaca, displays one of the few extant Aztec temples; the Spaniards systematically destroyed most Aztec buildings. This double-stairway pyramid was constructed over a similar earlier one built by the Tlahuica who were later subjugated by the Aztecs. Left: Plan of Teopanzolco.

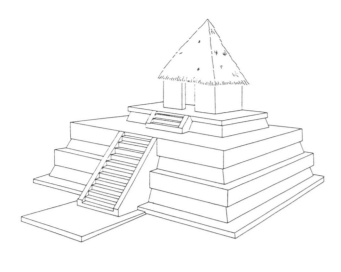

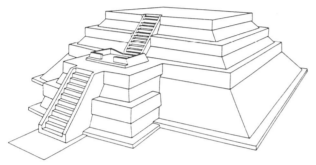

Below: The ruins of Kaminaljuyú lie within sprawling Guatemala City. Several tombs have been excavated, but none of the pyramids has been restored. Shown is the temple mound at Kaminaljuyú. Above: Reconstruction drawings of Buildings A-7 and B-4 show definite Teotihuacán influence.

The center of the great Aztec city of Tenochtitlán destroyed by the Spaniards in the early 1500s, now the Zocalo or Plaza de la Constitución of Mexico City. (From Heyden and Gendrop, p. 250).

METHODS OF RECOVERING THE PAST

How can a jungle-covered pile of masonry be made to reveal the secrets of its builders, perhaps dead hundreds of years before written history? The answer lies in the practice of archaeology, the study of the material remains of past human activities—artifacts, implements, burials, inscriptions, and constructions.

Pieces of pottery (sherds) have long been a key to interpreting the development of ancient civilizations. The sherds reveal the makeup of the pottery and the clay from which it was made as well as the kind and type of vessels being manufactured. Ceramic types and styles found in various strata can be employed to correlate the time frame in which the people lived and to some degree their level of cultural development. Archaeologists and art historians can recognize pottery from Teotihuacán or Tikal—or from most major and many minor sites—and determine approximately when it was fired. Sequences of ceramic styles and spatial linkages (horizons) covering most of Mesoamerica have been worked out.

Architecture, ceremonial centers, and urban settlement patterns are also valuable in determining the time during which a culture flourished. Most excavated Mesoamerican sites reveal an evolution in art and architecture from earliest settlement to abandonment.

Art forms often clearly identify cultures. Teotihuacán sculpture and painting are easily identified, and so is the painting on Maya walls and vases. Figurine styles can tell the experts the time and place of their origin.

The Maya and Zapotecs had a glyphic writing system, much of which can now be read. Mayanists can tell the names, dates of birth, accession, and death of kings, and the painted pottery reveals much of the daily life of the nobles. The Maya Long Count calendar can give us exact dates. The conquering Spaniards destroyed most of the books and other writings of Precolumbian peoples in Mesoamerica. However, many Spanish chroniclers wrote descriptions of the peoples they encountered and some missionaries felt compelled to record the very heathen customs and practices they were trying to stamp out. From these documents, stored in archives in Europe, ethnohistorians have gleaned a wealth of information to supplement the studies of archaeologists, art historians, and linguists.

Archaeologists often trench to bedrock at appropriate points on a site to determine the stratigraphic record and to indicate that nothing older lies beneath that point. By comparing the ceramics or artifacts found above bedrock (layer by layer, one group of sherds above another), archaeologists can determine the history of the people who lived at that site over the centuries.

Radiocarbon (C14) dating involves the laboratory determination of the approximate age of organic materials (a wooden lintel, for instance). This device has proved to be a valuable adjunct to stratigraphic and Maya calendrical dating.

Thus the Mesoamericanists have been able to give us a picture of the development of New World Indian

civilizations from early Preclassic times to the arrival of the Spaniards.

Our knowledge of Mesoamerican Precolumbian cultures continues to burgeon. The recent work of R.E.W. Adams at Río Azul in the jungle of northern Guatemala is an example. The mural paintings of glyphs reveal Río Azul to have been an outpost of the great Maya city of Tikal to the south and show that Classic Tikal was the capital of a regional-state and the center of one of the world's greatest ancient civilizations.

Adams's new evidence indicates the Teotihuacanos, from the Mexican highlands, arrived in Tikal in A.D. 360. The conquest monuments—four round altars—at Río Azul show the execution of that city's old rulers by conquerors from Tikal and Teotihuacán and the installation of the son of Tikal's king, Stormy Sky, as Río Azul's ruler in about A.D. 435. The record shows he brought with him two Teotihuacán advisors.

Río Azul's roots extend back to 100 B.C. In late Preclassic and early Classic times the city developed independently. This may explain why Tikal needed Teotihuacán's aid to take it over. Tikal-controlled Río Azul served to fix Tikal's northern frontier until the early 800s.

The revelations at Río Azul show Teotihuacán's heavy influence on the lowland Maya in early Classic times. Adams now feels that Teotihuacán was an active ally of the family of the Tikal ruler, Curl Nose, who replaced the former ruling family of Jaguar Paw. Teotihuacán was also active in guiding the destiny of Río Azul as a protector of Tikal's trade routes to the interior. These cities sit astride the principal river trade routes between the Maya lowlands and the Caribbean Sea.

At the time of the withdrawal of Teotihuacán from the Maya lowlands (around A.D. 535), Río Azul was abandoned for a time. The descendants of the Teotihuacán-backed Maya nobles later returned to power and the city continued to be the guardian of Tikal's frontier until it was overrun and burned by raiders from the Maya Puuc region of Yucatán in A.D. 830.

The evidence resulting from the archaeological research at Río Azul sheds new light on the role of Teotihuacán in the Maya lowlands in early Classic times and the regional power of the city of Tikal. It adds additional pieces of evidence necessary for the reconstruction of Mesoamerican civilizations.

Additional new light on the lowland Classic Maya comes from the work of Diane and Arlen Chase and others at Caracol, a large Maya site near the Belize border southeast of Tikal. The Chases discovered an altar inscribed in A.D. 633 by Lord Kan II of Caracol indicating the defeat of Tikal in A.D. 562 and the domination of Tikal for about 140 years. This revelation seems to explain the hiatus at Tikal that occurred between the middle 500s to 700. During this period at Tikal, there was a dearth of carved monuments, poor burials, and evidence of general hard times. Tikal's Lord Double Bird, who appears on Stela 17 at Tikal, is shown by Caracol's glyphs to have been defeated and taken prisoner and was probably humiliated, tortured, and executed as was the custom among the Maya rulers.

Additional glyphic evidence at Caracol indicates the conquest of other Maya sites by Caracol beginning in A.D. 800, which, coupled with the known hostilities by the Maya of Yucatán against the Maya cities of the Petén, adds another dimension—wars of conquest—to the collapse of the lowland Classic Maya civilization.

Opposite, above: Reconstruction drawing of Pyramid 15 at Río Azul. The city of Río Azul stood guardian of Tikal's north region. This 155-foot-high Classic Maya pyramid consisted of fourteen rubble-filled platforms. (Painting by Roy Anderson, © 1986 National Geographic Society). Below: Río Azul's looted tomb of Ruler X (a member of the royal family of Tikal who was born September 29, A.D. 417) is examined by R.E.W. Adams. (Photograph by George F. Mobley, © 1986 National Geographic Society).

CHAPTER ONE

Central Mexico

During the thousand years before the Christian Era, according to M. D. Coe, the Valley of Mexico was a prosperous but provincial backwater compared to the Preclassic Maya, Olmec, and Oaxacans to the east and south. The relative isolation of the valley continued into late Preclassic times, until about A.D. 150.

In ancient times five shallow, marshy, reed-lined lakes extended from south to north for about 35 miles in the basin of the Valley of Mexico. Surrounded on all sides by mountains, the valley covered approximately 600 square miles of the 7,000-foot-high, semiarid plateau that makes up central Mexico. In or very near this valley were built some of the great cities of all time: Teotihuacán, with a population approaching 200,000, rivaled its contemporary—ancient Rome; Tula, capital city of the Toltecs, flourished after the fall of Teotihuacán; and Tenochtitlán-Tlatelolco, the twin cities of the Aztecs, destroyed by the conquering Spaniards in the 1500s, and upon the ashes of which modern Mexico City arose to become the largest city in the Western world with a current population of 18 million.

Beginning before 1000 B.C., villages grew up around these lakes. They were small settlements populated by sedentary farmers growing corn, beans, squash, and chilies. Tlatilco (settled about 1200 B.C.) was a town-size settlement located on the west side of Lake Texcoco, the central and largest of the valley's lakes. Tlatilco's excavated burials have yielded sophisticated painted figurines of dancers and ballplayers as well as pottery dishes, bowls, and stirrup-spouted jars. The influence of the

Olmecs from the Gulf Coast can be seen in some of the pottery. However, only nineteen sites occupied during this early period (1300–800 B.C.) have been discovered, which suggests a low population.

About seventy-five late Zacatenco phase sites (800–600 B.C.) have been found, indicating a definite population increase. Each of these lakeshore villages housed from 1,000 to 2,000 people. The Olmec motifs that appeared earlier in the pottery had disappeared by this time.

By late Preclassic, pyramids with thatch-roof temples were being built in some of the larger villages that surrounded the lakes. The circular pyramid at Cuicuilco, located south of Mexico City, was one of the earliest and largest—65 feet high and 260 feet in diameter. Cuicuilco was a town of about 20,000 people when it, like Pompeii, was covered by lava from the Xictli volcano about A.D. 100. On the east side of the lakes and at the opposite end of the Valley of Mexico from Cuicuilco, Teotihuacán had already grown to cover nearly 3 square miles and house about 20,000 persons by A.D. 1.

Doris Heyden and Paul Gendrop suggest Mesoamerica created its own architectural language during Preclassic times: the superposition of bodies of earth and rubble to form stepped, truncated pyramids and cones became a pattern that endured for twenty-five centuries. M. D. Coe points out that these tiered platforms formed the nuclei of virtually all enlarged villages and towns in the valley by late Preclassic. Some of the platforms were faced with stone and coated with a thick layer of stucco, and some rose for several tiers. Thus the appearance of temple-pyramids marked the major social change from small villages of farmers with household figurines as religious symbols to hierarchical societies with rulers who could mobilize the populace to build and maintain temple-pyramids to honor and placate the gods. By the end of the Preclassic, the city of Teotihuacán dominated the Valley of Mexico. Here the Teotihuacanos laid out their gridded city and constructed the Pyramid of the Sun, the Pyramid of the Moon, and twenty temple complexes along the Street of the Dead. The city covered 8 square miles and housed between 80,000 and 120,000 people. Blanton and Kowalewski calculate that 80 to 90 percent of the total population of the valley resided in Teotihuacán.

The Classic stage of Mesoamerica, beginning between A.D. 150 and 300 and ending around A.D. 900, was one of the most dramatic times in civilization. While Western Europe was languishing in the Dark Ages, the Mexican plateau was flowering. The city of Teotihuacán became the beacon of civilization from the time of Christ to about A.D. 700, not only for central Mexico but for all of Mesoamerica.

After the collapse of Teotihuacán, central Mexico was dominated by the Toltecs of Tula until about A.D. 1150. When Tula was abandoned, the Toltecs moved south into the Puebla region to conquer and occupy Cholula.

On the southern fringe of the Valley of Mexico, southwest of modern Cuernavaca, the city of Xochicalco survived and flourished perhaps because of its location between the peoples in the Valley of Oaxaca to the south and those of Teotihuacán and Tula in the Valley of Mexico to the north.

When the Toltecs lost power in the 1100s, the Valley of Mexico was crowded with feuding city-states such as Atzcapotzalco, Colhuacan, and Xico. Onto this turbulent political scene appeared a militant and barbaric tribe from the north—the Aztecs, who were abhorred, resented, and rejected by the more civilized peoples of Mexico. After moving about in the Valley of Mexico for decades, the Aztecs were allowed to settle on some swampy islands near the west side of the great Lake of the Moon (Lake Texcoco) where they built two towns—Tenochtitlan and Tlatelolco. Thus, according to the legends, the Aztecs fulfilled the prophecy that they were to build a city where they saw an eagle sitting on a cactus and holding a snake in its mouth. This Aztec emblem now appears on the flag of Mexico.

By 1367 the warriors of the Tepanec kingdom of Atzcapotzalco, with the aid of Aztecs, conquered all the other city-states in the Valley of Mexico. When the Tepanecs in turn were overcome by the Aztecs 60 years later in A.D. 1426, Aztec dominance was established in central Mexico. The sanguinary Aztecs believed the sun/war god, Huitzilipochtli, required the hearts of sacrificial victims—particularly enemy warriors—to keep the sun in the sky. This idiosyncrasy on the part of the Aztecs, coupled with the concept of their destiny as the chosen rulers of Mexico, made them the scourge of Mesoamerica. The Aztecs were in many ways like the Romans: they were almost unbeatable militarists, accomplished builders, successful merchants; and they were able to absorb culture from more civilized peoples whom they dominated.

At the dedication of the Great Temple of Tenochtitlán, some 20,000 victims had beating hearts torn from their breasts to anoint the statues of the gods with human blood. After a group was sacrificed, their bodies were thrown down the temple stairways in view of the remaining victims and of the assembled Aztecs. Visiting chiefs from as yet unconquered neighboring city-states were also invited to attend. They were sumptuously housed and lavishly entertained while they watched the carnage of dedication. The Aztecs understood power politics.

By the time the Spaniards entered Mexico in 1519 the Aztecs had built a mighty empire administered from the city of Tenochtitlán that controlled much of Mesoamerica. Motecuhzoma Xocoyotzin (known generally as Moctezuma or Montezuma) was the emperor and in every sense served as an absolute ruler. During the last ten years of his reign, Moctezuma was terrified by predictions that his empire would be destroyed. Then he heard reports of great houses floating on the sea near the Gulf Coast; the houses were populated by strange men with white faces and long beards. Moctezuma was convinced these men embodied the god Quetzalcoatl and his army, for A.D. 1519 was also the Aztec year One Reed—the year of Quetzalcoatl's birth and the year his return from across the seas had been foretold. The Spaniards with their horses, cannons, war dogs, and the massive assistance of Indians from the coast whom the Aztecs had subjugated, marched into the highlands of Mexico where they were welcomed as gods into the city of Tenochtitlán. The emperor allowed himself to be kidnapped, and he died a prisoner of the Spaniards.

The powerful Aztec empire came to an end on August 13, 1521, when the last emperor, Cuauhtemoc, surrendered to the Spanish *conquistador* Hernan Cortez.

TEOTIHUACÁN

Teotihuacán's ruins, known to the Mexicans as the *Piramides*, lie about 45 miles northeast of Mexico City in an offshoot of the Valley of Mexico. This ancient city was one of the wonders of the Precolumbian New World and its ruins have been a source of admiration and awe

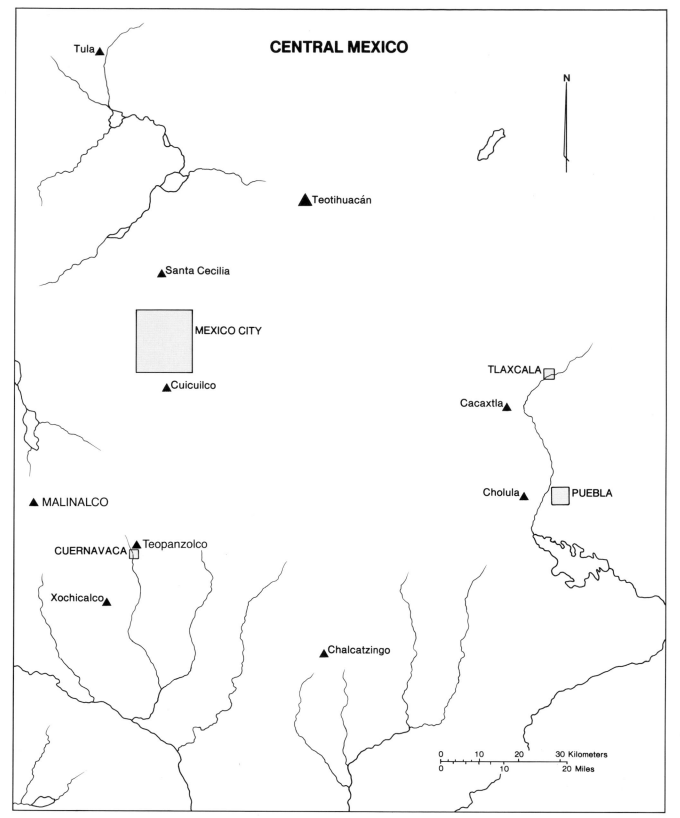

CENTRAL MEXICO

Tula▲

▲Teotihuacán

▲Santa Cecilia

MEXICO CITY

▲Cuicuilco

TLAXCALA◻

Cacaxtla▲

▲ MALINALCO

Cholula▲ ◻PUEBLA

CUERNAVACA◻ ▲Teopanzolco

Xochicalco▲

▲Chalcatzingo

N

| 0 | 10 | 20 | 30 Kilometers |
| 0 | | 10 | 20 Miles |

Surrounding modern Mexico City are a number of ancient Mesoamerican ruins included in this volume: Xochicalco, Teopanzolco, Chalcatzingo, Cholula, Cacaxtla, Teotihuacán, Malinalco, and Tula.

for 1,200 years. During its halcyon days it was a religious Mecca for much of Mesoamerica. Half a millennium after its fall the Aztecs named the city Teotihuacán ("the place where men become gods"), believing it was the place chosen by the gods to begin the fifth reincarnation (fifth sun) of the world. It was a place of pilgrimage for the Aztec lords who called the pyramid-lined north-south avenue between the Pyramid of the Moon and the Citadel, the Avenue of the Dead; they buried their lords along its way. The Aztecs rewrote their history to claim the Teotihuacanos were the ancestors of the Toltecs, from whom they—or at least their kings and nobles—were descended. Today the ruins remain a magnet for visitors from all over the world.

Widespread demand for obsidian (volcanic glass), mined in the hills and mountains near the village that was to become Teotihuacán, made it a major Precolumbian trade item during the two centuries before the Christian Era and probably served as the catalyst that turned Teotihuacán from a village of farmers into a city. A fist-sized piece of obsidian could be chipped into dozens of razor-sharp blades that never lost their edges. In 900 years, Teotihuacán grew from a large village of about 6,000 people into Mesoamerica's most influential city covering more than 8 square miles, with a population of at least 120,000 and possibly 200,000. An extensive mapping project led by Rene Millon has provided us with a relatively clear picture of the city's growth.

During the Teotihuacán I occupation (150–100 B.C. to A.D. 150), the Teotihuacanos began to build the great pyramids of the Sun and the Moon and platted the city into quadrants along two central perpendicular axes. The Avenue of the Dead formed the north-south axis with an orientation of 15° 28′ east of north, while the east-west street lay 16° 30′ north of west. Anthony F. Aveni has located three cross petroglyphs that he suggests acted as surveyor's marks. One mark near the Pyramid of the Sun forms one line with a second mark on a prominent hill to the north along the precise bearing as the Avenue of the Dead and another line with the third mark on another prominent hill to the west parallel to the east-west street. These two axial streets divided the city into four quarters centered on the Citadel.

The excavated portion of the Avenue of the Dead extends south from the Pyramid of the Moon beyond the huge Pyramid of the Sun only as far south as the Temple of Quetzalcoatl located within the Citadel. In ancient times the street extended twice as far. Lining both sides of this avenue stand a number of ruins (mostly temple platforms) that have also been partially restored. This core area served as the ceremonial and administrative center of the city. Rulers, chieftains, and pilgrims who came from all over Mesoamerica were probably awed by the religious grandeur of Teotihuacán. One testament to the commercial aspect of the city is the Great Compound marketplace, a complex of platforms and buildings built during the latter part of Teotihuacán II (A.D. 150–450) that covers an area larger than any other unit of construction in the city.

Rene Millon estimates that during Teotihuacán II, the city grew to a population of 20,000 or more. The pyramids of the Sun and the Moon were completed during these times as was the impressive Temple of Quetzacoatl in the Citadel. These buildings embodied the architectural technique of pyramidal platforms constructed with alternate sloping *taluds* and upright *tableros*. The masonry pyramids and buildings were covered with stucco and painted—some in solid colors, others with multicolored frescoes. Many buildings displayed painted frescoes both inside and out.

Teotihuacán's layout was unique in Mesoamerica; no other city was designed according to a predetermined grid plan before the Aztec city of Tenochtitlán. In addition to the great avenues that quartered the city, smaller streets and lanes framed residential compounds enclosed within walls about 185 feet square. Obviously the more elaborate palace compounds were the residences of the lords. One is the magnificent Palace of the Quetzal-Butterfly (with facades and columns decorated with low reliefs), located just southwest of the Pyramid of the Moon. The palaces contained 40 or 50 one-story rooms arranged around a sunken central court. The walls were decorated with multicolored frescoes of gods, animals, and gardens. One fresco depicts the Rain God's paradise with dancing figures and flowering trees effused with butterflies. No other Mesoamerican city had so many painted walls. Ignacio Bernal suggests the beauty of Teotihuacán's murals was only incidental to their religious symbolism.

Bernal also maintains that priests rather than kings and nobles made up the ruling class. Other important classes were the merchants who traded Teotihuacán's goods throughout Mesoamerica and regulated commerce, and the militia who insured the city's safety and position of dominance. The economy probably depended upon long-distance trade and management of a complex marketing system. This great city's influence spread from the Valley of Mexico to the Puebla Valley, Vera Cruz, Monte Albán, Xochicalco, Chiapas, the Maya lowlands, and Kaminaljuyú in the uplands of Guatemala. All of these regions evidence heavy Teotihuacán influence. Teotihuacán's beautiful bowls, dishes, vases, and masks have been found in elite burials throughout Mesoamerica.

Between A.D. 450 and 650 (Teotihuacán III), the city reached the peak of its prosperity and influence. Millon estimates it may have housed as many as 125,000 to 200,000 people. Bernal believes the government became more secular and political control shifted from the priests, if in fact the city-state was ever a true theocracy. M. D. Coe suggests an elite group of lords inhabited the zones now called Xolalpan, Tetitla, Tepantitla, Zacuala, Atetelco, and Quetzalpapalotl, (Palace of the Quetzal-Butterfly). The Citadel probably functioned as the royal palace.

Compounds containing more than 2,000 one-story apartments housed the common people. Some apartments consisted of several rooms built around unroofed patios and often included a small temple. There were areas for craft specialties such as ceramics, obsidian-working, stone work, the manufacture of feather headdresses, and the production of figurines. An immigrant group from the Valley of Oaxaca lived in its own compound, as did the Maya and possibly others.

By A.D. 600, Teotihuacán was a cosmopolitan city in every aspect, manifesting great power and influence over Mesoamerica. Then its light began to dim and like ancient Rome's dominance 200 years before, Teotihuacán's influence over its world waned and finally died. No one knows what precipitated the decline—perhaps it was the disruption of the trade routes by the rising power of Xochicalco and other cities. Adams suggests the city was destroyed around A.D. 540–550, when Teotihuacán withdrew from the lowlands—about the time Río Azul was burned; but most historians generally place the decline after A.D. 650. It is not certain who was responsible for Teotihuacán's destruction, where they came from, or why they destroyed the city. W. T. Sanders and J. Litvak King suggest that Tula, Xochicalco, Cholula, and other cities allied against Teotihuacán and succeeded in destroying the city.

We do not know who the inhabitants of Teotihuacán were, nor what language they spoke. The city was put to the torch about 750 and the palaces and temples along the Avenue of the Dead were burned. Squatters inhabited the ruined buildings of the city until about A.D. 900. The Aztecs in the 1400s venerated the ruins as a sacred and a ceremonial place. Most of the principal Aztec gods were worshiped at Teotihuacán: the Rain God (Tlaloc), the Feathered Serpent (Quetzalcoatl), Xipe Totec, the Old Fire God, the Water Goddess, the Sun God, and Moon Goddess.

Pyramid of the Sun Dedicated to the Sun God, this colossal mass was erected by men who carried about 1,500,000 cubic yards of sun-dried bricks and rubble on their backs—probably using tumplines. The pyramid, which was raised in stages during the first century A.D., measures 738 feet on each side and (including the temple on the top that has been destroyed) reached a

height of 249 feet. It was constructed over a natural cave, 23 feet deep and 328 feet long, which ended in a chamber shaped like a four-petaled flower, suggesting the pyramid was erected on sacred ground. Within the pyramid are the remains of an earlier pyramid. The small structure in front of the Pyramid of the Sun is an Aztec shrine erected hundreds of years after Teotihuacán had been abandoned.

At the turn of the twentieth century, Leopoldo Batres, thinking there was another well-preserved pyramid directly beneath the Pyramid of the Sun, cut about 23 feet off three sides of the pyramid. The west facade retains its original size and configuration. On the other three sides are the old retaining walls. Originally the entire exterior of the pyramid was covered with a thick layer of smooth plaster and painted—probably red. Bernal suggests that at one time the facade was adorned with sculptured stone figures and decorations similar to those on the facade of the Quetzalcoatl Temple.

Plaza of the Moon The partially restored Pyramid of the Moon stands at the north end of the Avenue of the Dead. In front of it, the 670- by 450-foot plaza is outlined with platforms that in ancient times were stuccoed, painted, and topped with temples. In the center of the plaza the Teotihuacanos erected a low platform where dances and ceremonials could be watched from the steps of the surrounding temple-pyramids. Although the Pyramid of the Moon is smaller than the Pyramid of the Sun, the difference in elevation makes them appear to be roughly equal in height. It, too, was completed in late Preclassic times (probably between A.D. 100 and 200 during the beginning of Teotihuacán II) and later enlarged.

Palace of the Quetzal-Butterfly This sumptuous palace lies to the west of the Plaza of the Moon. Restored after 1962 from a pile of rubble, the palace now presents a delight to visitors. Near the center is an open patio surrounded by heavy stone columns each carved with beautiful bas-reliefs displaying a quetzal-butterfly and various water symbols. The background of the cornices were painted red and adorned with symbols in white. This palace unquestionably was the residence of a very high ranking noble.

The Citadel The huge wall-enclosed compound that constitutes the Citadel, with its complex of temples and buildings, must have been the city's center of power and palace of the ruler. It was a huge quadrangle surrounded by a wide, elevated platform some 1,300 feet on a side, supporting fifteen small temple platforms. Walls once topped the embankments, giving security and privacy to the residents within.

The west side of the old Temple of Quetzalcoatl, the principal temple of Teotihuacán, displays one of the

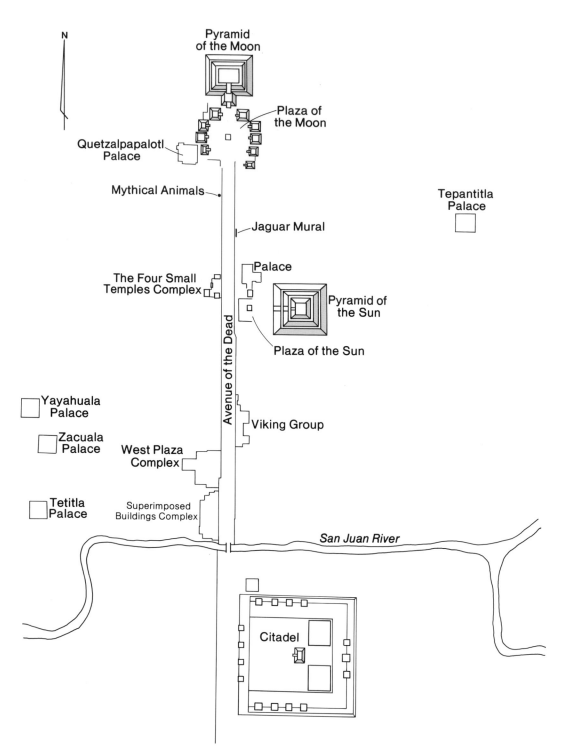

N

Pyramid
of the Moon

Plaza of
the Moon

Quetzalpapalotl
Palace

Mythical Animals

Tepantitla
Palace

Jaguar Mural

Palace

The Four Small
Temples Complex

Pyramid of
the Sun

Avenue of the Dead

Plaza of the Sun

Yayahuala
Palace

Viking Group

Zacuala
Palace

West Plaza
Complex

Tetitla
Palace

Superimposed
Buildings Complex

San Juan River

Citadel

The center of ceremonial Teotihuacán was the temple-lined, north-south avenue now referred to as the Avenue of the Dead. At the north end stands the Pyramid of the Moon and the Palace of the Quetzal-Butterfly, and to the south the Citadel. This area was only a small portion of the greatest city of Meso-america that may have housed some 200,000 people in its heyday.

most exciting facades in all Mesoamerica—a facade of *talud* and *tablero* panels decorated with carved, feathered serpents (Quetzalcoatl) and either the round-eyed Rain God, Tlaloc, or as Coe suggests, the Fire Serpent with an upturned snout. The background was painted blue. Sea shells have been carved on its surface. These magnificent carvings are well preserved because in Classic times the later Teotihuacanos covered this facade with a four-tiered *talud-tablero* temple-pyramid.

Above: The partially excavated Pyramid of the Moon at Teotihuacán stands at the north end of the Avenue of the Dead. Temples lined the avenue on both sides. Below: Pyramid of the Moon and plaza.

Above: The Teotihuacán Plaza of the Moon surrounds a large central platform. All the buildings are constructed in tiers with characteristic alternating framed tableros *(upright panels) and* taluds *(inclined panels). Below: The Palace of the Quetzal-Butterfly lies to the west of the Plaza of the Moon.*

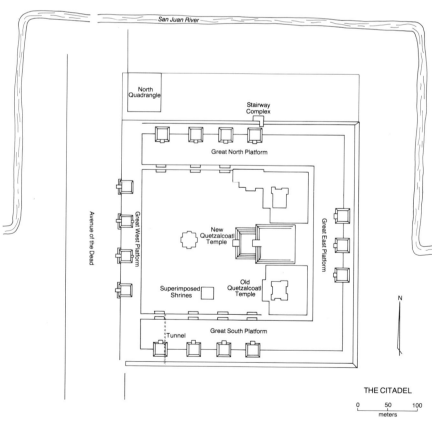

Above: The facade of the Teotihuacán Temple of Quetzalcoatl displays alternatively the heads of the plumed serpent (Quetzalcoatl) and—some archaeologists say—the round-eyed Rain God, Tlaloc. (Other archaeologists suggest it is the Fire Serpent with upturned snout). Within the panels are sea shells and rattlesnake rattles; between the panels serpents slither along. Left: Within a huge walled quadrangle, the Citadel contains the famous Quetzalcoatl Temple, palaces, and a complex of shrines and temples.

San Juan River

North Quadrangle

Stairway Complex

Great North Platform

Avenue of the Dead

Great West Platform

Great East Platform

New Quetzalcoatl Temple

Superimposed Shrines

Old Quetzalcoatl Temple

Tunnel

Great South Platform

N

THE CITADEL

0   50   100
meters

Above: Head of the plumed serpent on the facade of the Temple of Quetzalcoatl. Left: The central altar in the courtyard of the Atetelco Palace reproduces a miniature temple-pyramid. Atetelco ("the stone wall by the water") is a group of restored buildings on the west side of the Teotihuacán ruins.

Above: The patio of the Palace of the Quetzal-Butterfly is surrounded by square columns incised on three sides with bas-reliefs of the Teotihuacán deity, the Quetzal-Butterfly. Right: A corner of the patio of the Palace of the Quetzal-Butterfly. This palace was constructed in the shadow of Teotihuacán's Pyramid of the Moon.

Above: This mural painting at Tepantitla may represent a priest performing crop fertility rites. Below: The person (or deity) pictured on a mural at Tetitla combines qualities of Tlaloc (Rain God) and Quetzalcoatl (Feathered Serpent). Tepantitla lies to the east and Tetitla to the west of the Teotihuacán's Avenue of the Dead outside the core area.

Top: This mural painting at Tetitla on the west side of the Teotihuacán ruins depicts the frontal view of an owl with outstretched wings, exaggerated predatory claws, and prominent tail feathers. Middle: This painted bird at Tetitla may be a vulture (in profile). It grips a conch shell from which a speech scroll emerges. Left: A carved cat from Teotihuacán now in the British Museum collection.

Ballcourt 2

Altar

Central Plaza

This photographic panorama and schematic drawing of Tula's Central Plaza was taken from the Great Pyramid on the plaza's east side. In the center of the plaza stands an altar behind which are the ruins of the west ballcourt. The north side of the Central Plaza is bounded by the Burnt Palace and a pyramid topped with colossal warrior figures. The pyramid is variously named Tlahuizcalpantecuhtli, Temple of Quetzalcoatl, Pyramid of the Atlanteans, and Pyramid B.

TULA

Tollan of the Toltecs, and of Kings Topiltzin and Huemac, is now known to sit on a limestone promontory overlooking the town of Tula on the northwest edge of the Valley of Mexico. Because of its great reputation held by the later Aztecs as the home of the Toltecs, many archaeologists in the 1930s and 1940s assumed it must have been a huge city like Teotihuacán. Because Tula was burned in the A.D. 1100s and looted by the Aztecs of much of its undestroyed artwork in the 1300s and 1400s, and because only a small portion of Tula has been excavated, the visible ruins do not now appear to

reflect the grand ancient city with a peak population of 30,000 to 40,000. Thus it took several decades for scholars to agree these ruins are, in fact, ancient Tollan.

Following the fall of Teotihuacán, Tula, or Tollan of the Toltecs, became the dominant city in Mexico's central plateau. Located toward the northern frontier of Mesoamerica, Tula was occupied from about A.D. 800 until it was burned and sacked about 1150.

The Pyramid of Tlahuizcalpantecuhtli (or the Pyramid of Quetzalcoatl as the Morning Star, Pyramid B) is the most impressive excavated structure at Tula. It is a five-stepped pyramid topped by four colossal column-

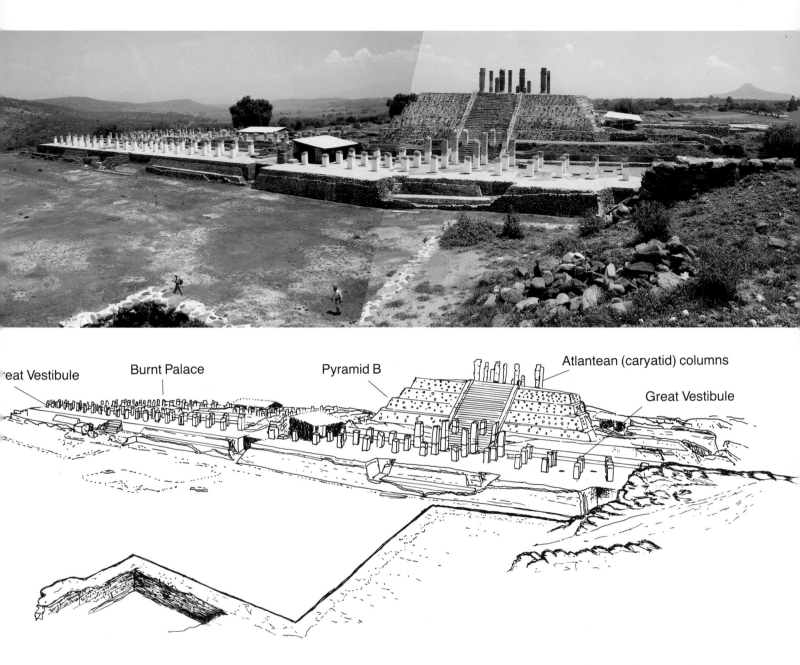

Great Vestibule   Burnt Palace   Pyramid B   Atlantean (caryatid) columns

Great Vestibule

like stone figures (not atlantes but often referred to as such) of Toltec warriors that originally functioned as supports for the roof of the temple. They were discovered in modern times broken into pieces on the ground north of the pyramid. Joined with the pyramid on the east side, several structures make up the Palace of Quetzalcoatl. The pyramid's base wall was adorned with bas-reliefs symbolizing warrior orders in the form of jaguars, coyotes, and eagles eating human hearts.

If the legends contained in the annals written in Spanish after the conquest are pieced together, we see a picture of Toltec society made up of Nahuatl-speaking Chichimecs—barbarians from the desert regions north of the Valley of Mexico. These Toltecs moved into the civilized regions of Mexico about A.D. 900. They were led by a semi-legendary ruler named Mixcoatl (Cloud Serpent). Mixcoatl's son, Ce Acatl Topiltzin Quetzal-

coatl (born just prior to 950), became the most famous figure of Precolumbian Mexico. Topiltzin claimed Quetzalcoatl, the feathered serpent deity, as his guardian and added the deity's name to his own. The annals also tell us that Tula society was torn by violent inner strife. As king, Topiltzin Quetzalcoatl preferred relative peace and abhorred human sacrifice. But devotees of the god Tezcatlipoca (Smoking Mirror), the patron of warriors, and a god who demanded human sacrifice, opposed him and drove him from Tula in 987. The legends of the Yucatec Maya and the archaeology of Yucatán indicate that about this time Chichén Itzá was conquered by Toltec invaders led by Kukulcán (Feathered Serpent in the Maya language). This king (Topiltzlin?) had fair skin, long hair, and a black beard. Five centuries later, the legend predicting Quetzalcoatl's return led the Aztec king Moctezuma (Montezuma) to assume the Spanish

Above: Tula. View across the plaza from the southwest showing the Great Pyramid (Building C), the Burnt Palace, and Pyramid of the Atlanteans. Left: A carved stone relief of a rattlesnake devouring a human skeletal figure.

Opposite: These huge stone columns of Tula's Pyramid of the Atlanteans once supported the roof of a temple on top of a stepped-pyramid. Each warrior carries an atlatl and sheaf of arrows, a butterfly breast plate on his chest, and a solar disc on his back.

conquistador Cortez fulfilled this prophecy. Thus the Aztec king's equivocations in dealing with the Spaniards contributed in no small measure to the Spanish victory and the destruction of Precolumbian Mesoamerican civilization.

The Tezcatlipoca warriors of Tula brought the city to its greatest size and power. From Tula the Toltecs controlled most of central Mexico, as well as parts of the highlands of Guatemala and the Yucatán Peninsula in the 150 years between A.D. 1000 and 1150. Later in

the 1400s Aztec nobles revered the ancient Toltecs and claimed descent from their rulers and gods.

The ruins are interesting and easily accessible, located only about 50 miles north of Mexico City. The excavated area covers only a small portion of the city—about 400 yards north to south by 275 yards east to west, not including the parking lot and museum. Nevertheless, from the tourist's point of view, in the Mexico City region only the ruins of Teotihuacán, Cholula, and Xochicalco surpass or equal Tula.

The Ruins of Tula from the Great Pyramid From the top of the largely unrestored Great Pyramid (Pyramid C) on the east side of the Central Plaza, the visitor can see to the north the Pyramid of the Atlanteans, with its warrior columns, and to its left the ruins of the Burnt Palace. Fronting the pyramid and palace in ancient times stood a huge, flat-roofed hall, now referred to as the Great Vestibule; all that remains of the hall is an L-shaped raised platform supporting dozens of stubbed columns.

Left: Tula. A carved jaguar above two eagles eating human hearts. Below: A feathered, forked-tongue deity resembling Tlaloc sits below a jaguar facing another animal, possibly a wolf or coyote.

Adjacent to the pyramid at the northeast corner lie the ruins of the Palace of Quetzalcoatl—perhaps the residence of Ce Acatl Topiltzin Quetzalcoatl. The palace ruins preserved one of Tula's extant jewels, the bas-relief panels along the base of the pyramid: a procession of alternating wolves and jaguars, below which ran a series of eagles eating bleeding hearts interspersed with full front expressions of the Rain God Tlaloc. On the north side of the pyramid's base is the Serpent Wall (Coatepantli): bas-reliefs and painted friezes depicting serpents eating human skulls (or perhaps skulls emerging from the serpents' mouths).

From the top of the Great Pyramid, one can look across Central Plaza to the west. In the center of the plaza is a small structure called the Altar, beyond which on the west side of the plaza sit the ruins of Ballcourt 2.

Excavated Ballcourt 1 lies to the north of the Pyramid of the Atlanteans–Burnt Palace complex.

One of the most interesting aspects of the ruins of Tula is its amazing architectural similarity to Chichén Itzá in northern Yucatán. The chacmool, a small statue of a human being with a flat place on the abdomen used as a receptacle for sacrificial human hearts, may be seen in the Tula museum and also at Chichén Itzá. The representations of warrior cults are common to both cities as are the flat-roofed, square-columned halls. A tour of both cities can leave little doubt that they were closely related.

Above: Tula. A carved wolf or coyote.

Below: Tula. Excised hearts of sacrificial victims were placed in the receptacle on the chacmool's stomach. (Photograph by Joyce Kelly).

Above: A panorama of the buildings surrounding the Patio of the Altars at Cholula. Opposite, below: South side of the great Pyramid of Cholula with the reconstructed Patio of the Altars at its base and topped by a Spanish Colonial church. The Pyramid, one of the largest in the New World, reached a height of more than 175 feet.

CHOLULA

On the plain to the east of the twin volcanoes Iztaccihuatl and Popocatepetl rises the Great Pyramid of Cholula (also called the Pyramid of Tepanapa), possibly the largest man-made edifice in the Precolumbian New World. At its top now sits the delicate little colonial church of Nuestra Senora de los Remedios. When study of the pyramid complex was begun in 1930, tunnels were dug into the mass from north to south and east to west revealing a series of superimposed pyramids. Other tunnels followed the contours of the buried buildings. Further investigation directed by Ignacio Marquina continued between 1966 and 1970.

Buried beneath the huge pile now visible lies the first pyramid started some time near the beginning of the Christian Era. Around its sides ran Teotihuacán *talud-tablero* construction, painted red, yellow, and black with designs resembling insects and stylized butterflies also in the Teotihuacán style. Later this earliest pyramid and its surrounding buildings were covered with tons of earth in the construction of a second pyramid, said to have been slightly larger than the Pyramid of the Moon at Teotihuacán. This, too, was covered by successive layers of earth until finally in Classic times a truncated, square pyramid-platform was completed—extending nearly 1,000 feet on each side covering an area of nearly 20 acres—with a smaller square platform on its top upon which ceremonial structures stood. Estimates of the total height of the structure vary between 170 and 214 feet. Florencia Muller suggests that by A.D. 500 a new Cholula ceremonial center had been begun west of

Above: Patio of the Altars, Cholula. Below: A portion of the Drunkards Mural, which is more than 150 feet long, found within the pyramid, depicts life-sized figures drinking. M. D. Coe suggests the potion may have been hallucinogenic (made from mushrooms or peyote) rather than alcoholic.

Cutaway model reconstruction of the Pyramid of Cholula showing the Stone Building on the west and the buildings of the Patio of the Altars on the south.

the Pyramid of Tepanapa in the area now occupied by the modern city of Cholula. Here the Cholulans built a great temple to Quetzalcoatl that was still in use when the Spaniards arrived. The Pyramid of Tepanapa was abandoned for ceremonial purposes by A.D. 700–800.

Along the south side of the pyramid, the restored Patio of the Altars forms a large three-sided plaza decorated by fret motifs supporting a wide *talud-tablero* panel with a double cornice. The plaza contains four altars, two of which display low-relief designs in the style of El Tajín. At the south end of the plaza, an Aztec shrine was constructed centuries after the abandonment of the ceremonial center. On the east and west sides of the plaza, deep cuts revealed several superimposed structures. In one of these at a depth of nearly 20 feet the archaeologists discovered a long panel showing nearly life-sized figures in a drinking scene. Ignacio Marquina suggests it depicts a planting or harvest ceremony and the participants are drinking pulque. M. D. Coe feels they may be drinking a hallucinogenic potion derived from mushrooms or even peyote.

The beautifully restored Stone Building at the center of the pyramid's west side represents the most carefully constructed segment at Cholula: three tiers with *taluds* topped by deep *tableros*, all of perfectly cut and

fitted stone blocks covering the rubble fill. All other known construction at Cholula consisted of rubble or adobe fill covered only by a layer of small stones faced with stucco or clay.

The Cholula Museum displays a cutaway model showing the Patio of the Altars and other buildings on the south side of the pyramid, the stone *talud-tablero* building on the west, the earlier inner pyramids, and the church at the summit.

Cholula flourished in Classic times along with Teotihuacán, Monte Albán, and the Maya sites of Tikal and Copán; but later its focus shifted westward to the newer Temple of Quetzalcoatl during the Postclassic when Tula, and later Tenochtitlán, dominated Central Mexico.

Above: Reconstructed Stone Building on the west side of the Pyramid of Cholula.
Below: Rubble construction marking an earlier building stage on the north side of
the Stone Building.

XOCHICALCO

This fortified city, built upon a series of hills southwest of modern-day Cuernavaca, has roots back to 200 B.C. The ruins represent an occupancy (with a peak population of perhaps 20,000) from A.D. 700 to 1000. Xochicalco began to flower about the time of the Teotihuacán collapse, and the Classic Maya stage ended about midway through Xochicalco's golden age. The city was a trading center and one of calendrical-mathematical knowledge. It was located on the trade route between the Valley of Mexico and the regions to the south and east along which cotton, cacao, feathers, jade, and obsidian were carried. Xochicalco replaced Teotihuacán as a dominant trading center between the plateau of Mexico and the Valley of Oaxaca, the Gulf Coast, and the Maya lowlands.

M. D. Coe and R.E.W. Adams suggest Xochicalco was heavily influenced and may at times even have been ruled by the Classic lowland Maya. There is also evidence of strong ties to Monte Albán to the south and El Tajín on the Gulf Coast to the east. This merger of Mayan, Oaxacan, and Gulf Coast influence formed a cultural bridge in the Mexican highlands between Classic Teotihuacán and Postclassic Tula.

Temple of the Feathered Serpent   The ruin of the Temple of the Feathered Serpent in the Main Plaza constitutes the most singular and well-preserved architectural feature of Xochicalco. The temple, a square platform with a high *talud-tablero*, is covered with sculptured feathered serpents, stylized shells, bar-and-dot numbers, and Maya-like human figures. Heyden and Gendrop report that this fascinating building was erected to commemorate the New Fire ceremony, at the close of one of the 52-year cycles that marked the coincidence of the two Mesoamerican calendars—the solar version of 365 days and the ritual calendar of 260 days. Xochicalco's rulers may have organized an important congress of astronomers that was attended by many prominent Maya.

Along the base of the Temple of the Feathered Serpent is a sculpted relief of a feathered serpent whose undulating coils enshroud a number of figures seated and dressed in Maya fashion. Coe points out that one figure's name is given Teotihuacán-style as 9 Wind, the birthdate of the god Quetzalcoatl. He also notes there is no prototype for these Maya-like figures in highland Mexico, but they are very similar to the depictions of Classic Maya lords. The undulating serpent reliefs remind one of the low reliefs on the Temple of Quetzalcoatl at Teotihuacán.

Inscribed dates from Xochicalco show stylistic connections with Teotihuacán and Monte Albán. The causeways are similar to those at Tikal and the sculpture recalls El Tajín. Near the Temple of the Feathered Serpent is a cave that appears to be an observatory composed of a vertical man-made shaft through which a beam of sunlight shines on the cave floor when the sun stands directly overhead. Coe suggests some of the inscribed figures, the observatory, and the I-shaped ballcourt similar to that of Copán manifest Maya influence.

Temple of the Three Stelae   To the south of the Temple of the Feathered Serpent is the Temple of the Three Stelae. In 1961 three stelae were found in the rubble near the temple and later removed to the National Museum of Anthropology and History in Mexico City. They were carved with glyphs and numerals from the Nahuatl, Maya, and Zapotec cultures. Around A.D. 650, representatives from various Mesoamerican cultures assembled at Xochicalco for the purpose of adopting or consolidating a calendar. Heyden and Gendrop suggest that when the data carved on the stelae were no longer considered useful, the monuments were painted red (the color of death), ceremonially killed by breaking, and buried to lie undisturbed until the twentieth century.

Other Features   To the north of the Temple of the Feathered Serpent lies the observatory and westward across the plaza lies a huge unexcavated mound. From this mound the Temple of the Three Stelae can be seen to the south of the Temple of the Feathered Serpent. Next to it stands a large unexcavated pyramid overlooking a smaller plaza to the south on which are two partially restored temples—one on the east and one on the west with a platform and stela in the center.

Below the Xochicalco acropolis lie the ruins of the Maya-like 200-foot-long I-shaped ballcourt, the Palace (a residential area), and a partially excavated pyramidal mound called La Malinche.

Temple of the Feathered Serpent

Temple of the Three Stelae

Above: Temple of the Feathered Serpent, Temple of the Three Stelae, and the Plaza of the Stela of Two Glyphs, Xochicalco. Below: Schematic drawing of the Xochicalco ruins.

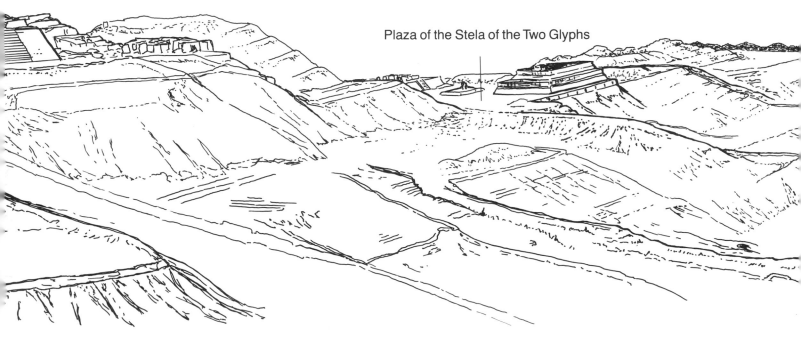

Plaza of the Stela of the Two Glyphs

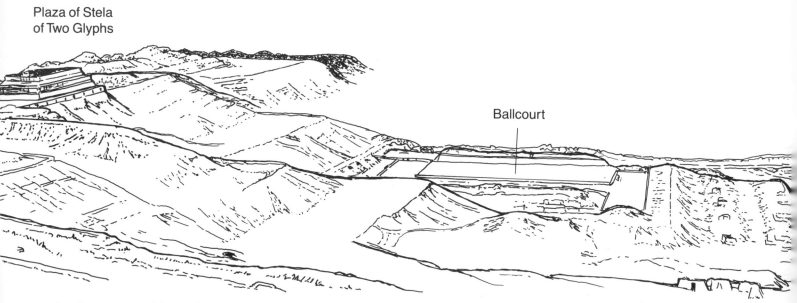

Plaza of Stela
of Two Glyphs

Ballcourt

Southern section of the Xochicalco ruins. From left to right: Plaza of Stela of Two Glyphs, ballcourt and circular platforms, and La Malinche.

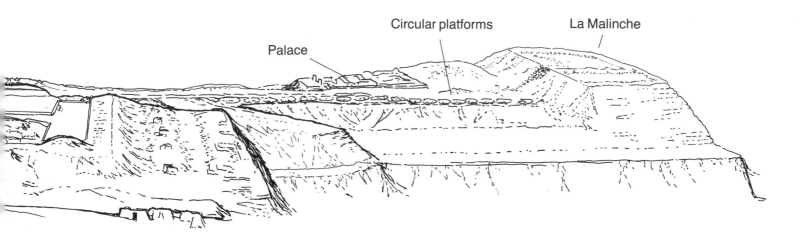

Palace

Circular platforms

La Malinche

Above: North facade of the Temple of the Feathered Serpent. Left: Feathered Serpent surrounding the symbol of what may have been the joining of the Meso-american solar (365-day) calendar and the ritual (260-day) calendar on the west side of the Temple of the Feathered Serpent, Xochicalco.

Detail representation of the ruler Three Flower.

Maya-like figure, sitting tailor-fashion, surrounded by coils of the Feathered Serpent on the north wall of the Temple of the Feathered Serpent, Xochicalco.

On the facade of the Temple of Feathered Serpent, Xochicalco. Above: Representation of a corn plant. Left: Detail of the connection of the solar and ritual calendars.

Above: Plaza of the Stela of Two Glyphs. Below: Ballcourt at Xochicalco with the Palace and La Malinche pyramid in the background.

Above: The Aztec Temple of the Eagle and Jaguar Knights at Malinalco, located about 40 miles by road northwest of Xochicalco, was carved out of the living rock. The modern conical thatched roof probably resembles the original. The city was conquered by the Spaniards in 1521. (Photograph by Lawrence G. Desmond). Left: On the right side of the Malinalco temple portal is an eroded sculpture of an Eagle Knight seated on top of a serpent's head. (Photograph by Lawrence G. Desmond).

Model of the excavated portion of the top of the pyramids at Cacaxtla (Cacaxtla Museum). The magnificent murals are beneath the roofed portion at the top.

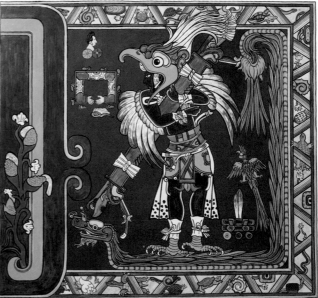

Top: Recently discovered Cacaxtla, a late Classic site in the Mexican highlands near Tlaxcala, displays Maya-like murals. Above: Cacaxtla mural, suggested reconstruction. (Painting by Jim Cruse).

Cacaxtla, battle scene between jaguar and feather-clad warriors.
Below: figure with eagle feet.

CACAXTLA

R.E.W. Adams feels that Cacaxtla, as well as Xochicalco, were hybrid cultures occupied in part by migrant military mercenaries, possibly Maya, who operated in the same manner as the Italian *condottieri* of the fourteenth and fifteenth centuries. These mercenaries may have taken over Cacaxtla and Xochicalco as intrusive elite rulers. Donald McVicker suggests that the Prehispanic murals found at Cacaxtla, a Classic site in the Mexican highlands near the city of Tlaxcala, were not merely influenced by the late Classic Maya, but were in fact painted by Maya artists. Xochicalco, El Tajín, Cholula, and Cacaxtla rose to prominence following the fall of Teotihuacán, and each displays influence from both highland and lowland Mesoamerica. This suggests a possible thrust of Classic Maya into the Mexican highlands. There was a Maya enclave at Teotihuacán before its fall, and strong evidence exists for Maya presence at both Xochicalco and Cacaxtla.

Reconstruction of El Tajín. (Painting by Richard Schlect, © 1980 National Geographic Society).

Cacaxtla, a late Classic fortified city, has approaches protected by defensive moats. M. D. Coe suggests it may have been inhabited by the Olmeca-Xicallanco described by the early chronicler Diego Munoz Camargo. Apparently, during late Classic and early Postclassic times people were moving in opposing directions: lowland Maya to the Mexican highlands, and highland Mexicans (Toltecs from Tula) to Yucatán in the lowlands.

Mary Ellen Miller (1986) describes the two prominent paintings in Building A as "stela-like portraits." One depicts a Maya in bird costume and the other a Maya in a full jaguar suit. She describes the bloody battle scene in Building B as central Mexican warriors in jaguar costumes defeating and mutilating Mayan warriors in bird suits. The scene may describe an actual battle or it may represent a mythical struggle between two political or religious factions showing the jaguar-aspect god (Tezcatlipoca) defeating the bird-aspect god (Quetzalcoatl)—part of the same myth surrounding the departure of Topiltzin Quetzalcoatl from Tula for the Toltec conquest of Chichén Itzá.

EL TAJÍN

El Tajín, the most spectacular Veracruz site, nestles among the rolling green hills about 10 miles south of the oil patch town of Poza Rica, Mexico. Although occupied since the Preclassic, it did not blossom until A.D. 600 to 900 in late Classic times. The core of the ancient city covered some 150 acres, but there were many outlying settlements. Here, as in most Precolumbian ruins, only a small portion of the original city has been excavated. The magnitude of El Tajín's ceremonial center during its halcyon days is captured in the painting by Richard Schlecht for the *National Geographic*: brightly painted temples in red and blue, great plazas, palaces, markets, an acropolis, and ballcourts constructed on artificial fills and manually leveled terraces.

The Pyramid of the Niches is El Tajín's best-known excavated building. The four-sided pyramid was built in six tiers, each one containing a number of small, square niches totaling 365—the number of days in the solar year. The presently visible structure covers an almost identical earlier building, also with 365 niches. To the north stands a cluster of excavated buildings decorated with step-and-fret motifs called Tajín Chico.

M. D. Coe writes, "Above all, the inhabitants of El Tajín were obsessed with the ballgame, human sacrifice, and death, three concepts closely interwoven in the Mexican mind" (Coe 1984:111). For some time archaeologists believed El Tajín had been built by the Totonacs, but we now know they migrated into this region late in the history of the city. The culture is now referred to as either "El Tajín" or "Veracruz." The city did not collapse at the end of Classic times (A.D. 800–1000) as many other Precolumbian cities did, but it continued to flourish until the early 1200s when it may have been destroyed by the Chichimecs, barbarians from the northwest.

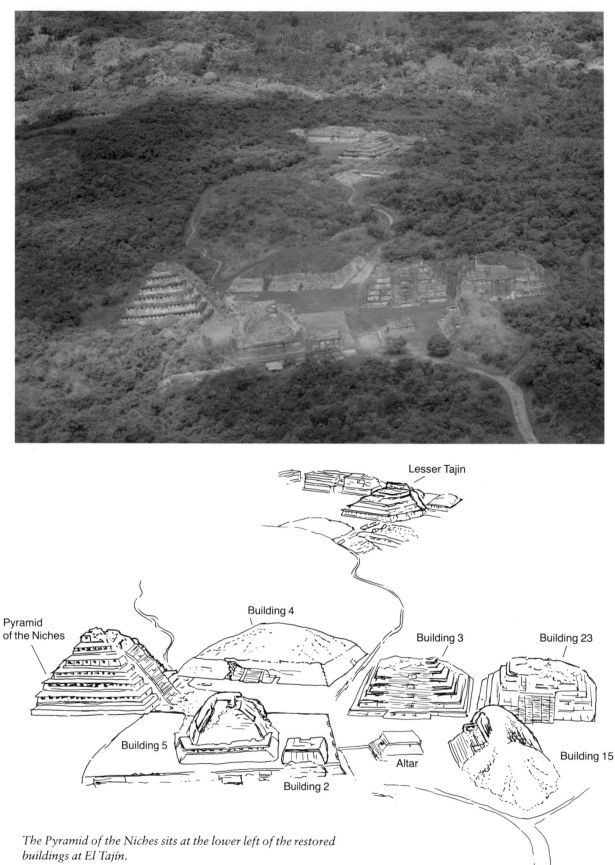

The Pyramid of the Niches sits at the lower left of the restored buildings at El Tajín.

Lesser Tajín buildings at El Tajín.

Building C at Lesser Tajín.

Step-and-fret design of Building D at Lesser Tajín.

Above: Pyramid of the Niches, El Tajín. (Photograph by Joyce Kelly). Below: Stela of the Death God, El Tajín.

The Olmec frontier site, Chalcatzingo, has an unexcavated pyramid surrounded by three volcanic cones that mark the site.

CHALCATZINGO

This curious Preclassic Olmec-style site lies in the Mexican highlands between Cuernavaca and Puebla to the south of the great mountain Popocatepetl. Archaeologists disagree about the kind and extent of the Olmec incursion into the highlands. Were they conquerors or only traders or missionaries? David C. Grove favors the idea of the Olmec influence through trade and marriage alliances rather than by military takeover.

The site is located at the foot of three 1,000-foot volcanic cones considered sacred by the Aztecs and probably also by the ancients. The ruin consists of platform mounds and terraces next to the base of the central mountain. Probably founded about 1500 B.C., Chalcatzingo reached its apogee between 700 and 500 B.C., making it contemporaneous with La Venta in the Olmec heartland on the Gulf Coast. The most curious and exciting facet of the ruin is a series of Olmec bas-reliefs on the cliff face and on several large boulders. The most impressive depicts a woman ruler enthroned in a stylized cave, or monster's mouth, with clouds floating out of it.

Chalcatzingo, south of Puebla, is an ancient Preclassic site with Olmec bas-reliefs.
The shrine is located on the talus slope about a third of the way up the mountain.

Monument 1, El Rey (named for the ruler figure), depicts the famous middle Preclassic woman ruler of Chalcatzingo seated on a throne within a cave symbolizing the Earth Monster mouth.

Monument 5 at Chalcatzingo consists of a bas-relief showing a human figure in the open mouth of the Feathered Serpent.

CHAPTER TWO

Valley of Oaxaca

Modern Oaxaca lies at the junction of three valleys in the mountains about 300 miles south of Mexico City. The three valleys form a sort of inverted-Y (aligned from the northwest to the southeast) where a major cultural center remained viable for thousands of years. To the west of Oaxaca stands a 1,300-foot mountain, the top of which has been flattened with prodigious human labor to construct one of Mesoamerica's most monumental ceremonial centers—Monte Albán. Down the Pan-American Highway, southeast toward the Isthmus of Tehuantepec, lie the ruins of Yagul, Dainzú, Zaachila, Lambityeco, and Mitla.

Monte Albán's Historical Periods

Early-Middle Preclassic   1500–500 B.C.
   Valley occupied. San José Mogote village has 400 people.

Monte Albán I   500–200 B.C.
   Masonry buildings, Danzantes, Zapotecan glyphic writing, bar-and-dot numerals, 52-year Calendar Round. Monte Albán becomes capital of the valley with up to 20,000 people.

Monte Albán II   200 B.C.–A.D. 300
   Population declines slightly. Conquests outside valley. Building J with conquest slabs constructed.

Monte Albán IIIA   A.D. 300–500
   Classic period begins; 200 villages and towns in the valley. Monte Albán itself has up to 22,000 inhabitants and its buildings are stuccoed and painted.

Monte Albán IIIB   A.D. 500–750
   Monte Albán reaches peak with up to 30,000 people and last major construction.

Monte Albán IV   A.D. 750–1000
   Monte Albán abandoned. Mitla becomes the Zapotec capital.

Monte Albán V   A.D.1000–1520
   Mixtec domination of valley. Mitla and Yagul rebuilt.

By 1500 B.C. (middle Preclassic), small farming villages were located throughout the valley, especially on the lower slopes of the mountains. The inhabitants, who grew maize, avocados, beans, and squash, lived in wattle-and-daub houses. Five hundred years later, an elite class began to appear; its members lived in larger houses built of stone and adobe. Burial sites that contained Olmec-style ceramics, displaying were-jaguar motifs, indicate a connection to the east with the Olmec heartland at San Lorenzo and La Venta. San José Mogote, an important valley regional center, had full-fledged masonry ceremonial buildings. In the mountains along the east side of the valley, crops were irrigated on artificially terraced hillsides.

Monte Albán, one of Mesoamerica's first real cities, was begun about 500–450 B.C. by the Zapotecs and served as the capital of the Oaxaca Valley until the end of Monte Albán IIIB. The entire valley was heavily populated from very early times, and it is literally covered with the remains of ancient communities. Richard Blanton has organized detailed surveys of the region that indicate full-time farmers existed in the valley 1,000 years before Monte Albán sprang up and nomadic hunters had foraged here for thousands of years before that. Until nearly the end of Monte Albán IV (about A.D. 900), the people of the valley were subject to few disruptions from outside because of their relatively isolated position. For 1,500 years the Valley of Oaxaca was the heart of a Zapotecan state, a continuously stable entity protected by mountains much as ancient Egypt was protected by deserts.

The Mixtecs came from the Mixteca, a mountainous region in the northwestern portion of the modern state of Oaxaca. Beginning about the middle 800s, they built a small empire by subjugating smaller neighboring states. By A.D. 1350, the Mixtecs had moved into the Valley of Oaxaca. By A.D. 1550, the Mixtecs had moved into the Valley of Oaxaca, and began conflict with the Zapotecs. They had taken over most of the one-time Zapotec sites by the time the Spaniards arrived in the 1500s.

Because of the amazing survival of eight Precolumbian codices (the Spaniards destroyed most of the others), particularly the Vienna Codex, some Mixtec dynasties can be traced; these codices show how the rulers of Mixteca were able to spread and consolidate their power by conquest and royal marriages.

MONTE ALBÁN

The Zapotec people who occupied the Valley of Oaxaca around 500 B.C. chose a central location on a high escarpment to build their capital. We believe it was designed to be an administrative city because the immediately adjacent slopes were unsuitable for farming. Even drinking water had to be laboriously carried up the mountain on the backs of men, for before the arrival of the Spaniards no Mesoamerican had a usable wheel or beast of burden. So the occupants of Monte Albán obtained their food from farms in the surrounding valleys. The burials tell us the inhabitants of Monte Albán were an elite ruling class. Within 200 years the city grew to 5,000 inhabitants and eventually reached 25,000 in Classic times.

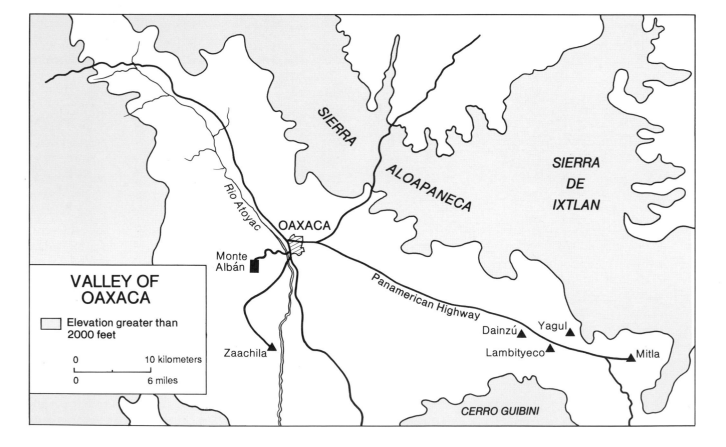

VALLEY OF OAXACA

Elevation greater than 2000 feet

0 — 10 kilometers
0 — 6 miles

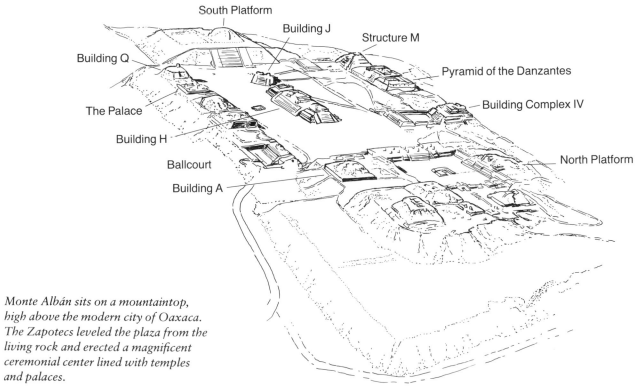

South Platform

Building J

Structure M

Building Q

Pyramid of the Danzantes

The Palace

Building Complex IV

Building H

Ballcourt

North Platform

Building A

Monte Albán sits on a mountaintop, high above the modern city of Oaxaca. The Zapotecs leveled the plaza from the living rock and erected a magnificent ceremonial center lined with temples and palaces.

Above: The late Preclassic Danzantes are believed to represent captives or slain enemies of the rulers of Monte Albán. Many are not in their original positions. Right: Bas-reliefs of Monte Albán's famous Danzantes inscribed during Monte Albán I (Preclassic) by the Zapotecs. Below: The Zapotecs developed the first literary texts in Mexico, such as these glyphic inscriptions including the bar-and-dot numerals. The bar was equal to 5 and the dot was equal to 1.

Above: The Temple of the Danzantes (dancers) was one of the oldest constructions at Monte Albán. The stone slabs carved with Danzantes may be seen at the base of the pyramid in the lower left. Below: Building J, thought to have been an observatory, sits at the south end of the Great Plaza immediately in front of the South Platform. Built about the beginning of the Christian Era, it displays glyphs representing people conquered by the Zapotecs of Monte Albán.

The Great Plaza of Monte Albán from the north. The foreground is dominated by the quadrangular North Platform. On the east side (left) of the plaza lie the ballcourt and the Palace.

Great Plaza of Monte Albán from the south. Along the west side of the plaza (left) stand the Temple of the Danzantes in the center flanked by Group IV on the north and Pyramid M on the south.

The Danzantes gallery of carved-stone monuments (some 350 of them) seems to have been the first building begun during early Monte Albán I. M. D. Coe has concluded these figures represent dead chiefs or kings captured and sacrificed by the early rulers of Monte Albán; their likenesses were engraved on stone slabs as proof of conquest. Many prehistoric societies, such as the Maya and the Peruvian Moche and Nazca, engaged in humiliation, torture, and execution of captured enemy rulers. These conquest slabs exhibiting executed enemy rulers indicate Monte Albán was a very important site, doubtlessly the power center of the valley. Such a display of terror tactics probably helped enforce the city's authority over the valley.

Monte Albán was one of the first political states in Mesoamerica to encompass a sizable surrounding hinterland. The city and its environs boasted more than 10,000 people by 350 B.C. Within the city stood elabo-

rate residences and public buildings indicating the existence of nobles who probably claimed descent from the gods. There is evidence of specialization in the production and marketing of pottery similar to the capitalist-style society that appeared later all over Mesoamerica. It was not free enterprise as we understand it, but rather a state-sponsored system of craft manufacture and marketing. Monte Albán's strategic location probably allowed it to subjugate the other, smaller states in the Valley of Oaxaca.

The arrowhead-shaped platform (Building J) in the south end of the Great Plaza seems to represent the Monte Albán II equivalent of the Danzantes gallery, for set in the sides of the building are forty carved stone slabs commemorating military conquests. Several alignments of this building suggest the Zapotecs placed some significance on the sun's passage through the zenith. By the end of Monte Albán II the Great Plaza had begun to

look something like it does today. The top of the mountain had been leveled into a plaza by cutting away solid rock peaks and filling the depressions—a Herculean task performed entirely by hand with stone tools.

During Monte Albán IIIA, the Valley of Oaxaca was heavily influenced by Teotihuacán culture and trade, as was every other culture in Mesoamerica; but it continued to function as an independent political and cultural entity.

The final period of construction around the Great Plaza occurred during Period IIIB (after A.D. 500). The plaza was completely enclosed by a series of stepped platforms, supporting temples and palatial residences. A ballcourt occupied the northeast corner. The huge South Platform enclosed the south end, and the very extensive North Platform supported a complex of courtyards and elite residences inaccessible to the common people. Many of these stone buildings have been partially re-

stored. The entire plaza complex was virtually sealed off making it a sacred area. During Monte Albán IIIB, the city reached a population of some 30,000. The stone masonry buildings were stuccoed and beautifully painted, making Monte Albán in A.D. 600 a dazzling city to behold. But by A.D. 750, after 1,200 years, the Main Plaza was abandoned, except for occasional ceremonies or elite burials. The Zapotecs occupied the Valley of Oaxaca for several more centuries and resisted the ever-encroaching Mixtecs; but the grandeur of Monte Albán had vanished. After the Mixtec takeover of Oaxaca, Zapotec burial sites and tombs were utilized by the Mixtec kings. One noble was buried with an amazing display of wealth: gold, silver, turquoise, and pearls. The contents of one of these opulent tombs (Tomb F), including a dazzling display of gold ornaments, is displayed in the museum at Oaxaca.

The doorway decoration above Tomb 104 at Monte Albán depicts a seated ruler wearing the headdress of the Zapotec Rain God, Cocijo.

This group of stelae lined a corner of the South Platform at Monte Albán during its Classic stage (Monte Albán III).

The ruins of ancient Mitla are now surrounded by the modern village of Mitla in the valley southeast of the city of Oaxaca. In the middle foreground is the excavated Group of the Columns.

MITLA

The modern town of Mitla has largely engulfed the ruins of ancient Mitla. The site was originally occupied by the Zapotecs, but the principal restored portions of the ruins were built by the later Mixtecs: a Mixtec palace (in the midst of which a colonial Catholic church was later built) and the Group of the Columns. Mitla became the capital of the Valley of Oaxaca in Monte Albán IV times.

The mosaic stonework of the ancient buildings of Mitla is incredible. Stepped-fret patterns, originally brightly painted, decorated the interior walls of sumptuous Mixtec palaces built during Monte Albán V.

The name Mitla seems to have derived from the Nahuatl word *mictlan*—"place of the dead." It probably originated in the reports of Father Burgoa, who found beneath the buildings at Mitla a huge catacomb where kings and nobles had been buried. He visited Mitla in the 1600s and wrote a detailed report describing the city as the residence of high priests, more powerful than the local kings, and as a center for human sacrifice.

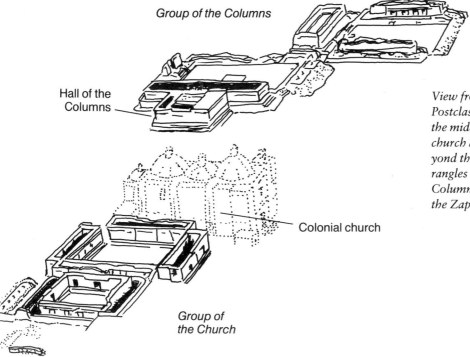

Group of the Columns

Hall of the
Columns

Colonial church

*Group of
the Church*

View from the east of Mitla, a Postclassic Zapotec and Mixtec city. In the middle foreground next to the church are the Church group ruins. Beyond the Colonial church are two quadrangles making up the Group of the Columns. Mitla was the burial place of the Zapotec kings and nobles.

Above: The exterior of the Palace in Group of the Columns at Mitla shows the Mixtec stepped-fret designs, probably the finest in all of Mesoamerica. Below: Entrance to the Hall of the Columns, Mitla.

Four detailed examples of the stepped-fret design from the Mitla Palace of Columns.
These mosaics were laid first and then painted.

Yagul, just east of the Pan-American Highway southeast of Oaxaca, shows an excavated ballcourt, temples, and palaces.

YAGUL

Yagul sits in beautiful surroundings backed against the mountains on the northeast side of the Tlacolula arm of the Valley of Oaxaca about 20 miles down the Pan-American Highway from the modern city of Oaxaca. Its occupation stretches back to Monte Albán I and probably further, even to preceramic times, and continues until the Spanish conquest. Like Mitla the early construction was Zapotec, followed by Mixtec stepped-fret facades similar to but not so refined as those at Mitla.

Four tombs have been discovered with Monte Al-

bán I period burials. The tombs are structurally similar to contemporary Monte Albán tombs except that they are made of adobe rather than stone. During Monte Albán IIIB and IV times, Yagul was occupied by the Zapotecs. In late Postclassic times the Mixtecs built over the earlier structures so that the ruins now visible are partially Zapotec and partially Mixtec.

On the hillside above the ruins of Yagul is the Great Fortress. Here are ruins of a fortified wall as well as platforms, plazas and tombs, and what may have been a lookout tower.

The acropolis abutting the mountain served as living quarters for the nobles. The ruins of these elite resi-

The Yagul acropolis sits on a promontory overlooking the Valley of Oaxaca. The valley was farmed in ancient times much as it is today.

dences are called the Palace of the Six Patios. To the south and below the palace is a beautifully restored ball-court, while west of it stands Patio 1 and the Council Hall, on the back of which is a stepped-fret decorated panel over 120 feet long. At both Yagul and Mitla the structures appear to have had a predominantly civic or public nature in contrast to the ceremonial structures at Monte Albán.

Partially restored portion of the Palace of Six Patios, Yagul.

Yagul's ballcourt is the largest in the Oaxaca Valley.

Triple tomb entrance with the doorway flanked by stone heads, Yagul.

DAINZÚ

Dainzú was not discovered until the 1960s and the area restored represents only a small portion of the site. Dainzú's principal attraction is its bas-relief carvings. These almost life-size figures are fitted into the wall of the stairway and into the lower tier of the north-facing building abutting the mountain. These carvings on inlaid stones, similar to the Danzantes at Monte Albán, depict gods, anthropomorphic jaguar figures, and ballplayers. The figures, which may have been carved as early as 300 B.C., suggest an Olmec origin, but were installed here at a much later time—probably not until the A.D. 600s. The ballcourt was not built until A.D. 1000.

Actually we know relatively little about the size or importance of Dainzú except that it was occupied, perhaps continuously, from very early times—possibly 700 B.C.—until historic times (some 2,200 years total) and that it probably was the capital of one of several competing small states in the valley. The excavations reveal a series of platforms and other structures built one over another, and the various styles of ceramics discovered in the excavated tombs confirm the long occupation.

The periods of occupancy at Dainzú and many other Mesoamerican sites cover mind-boggling expanses of time. Compared to European history the sequence would equal the time span from the post–Roman Byzantine Empire in the east, the Vandals in Spain, the Franks in France, and the Anglo-Saxon kingdoms in Britain until today. More than that, Dainzú may have been occupied another 500 years until the Spaniards arrived, which would, by comparison, push the start of our time span analogy back to the beginnings of Rome.

Here, as at Monte Albán, large, incised stone slabs display the figures. Most of the figures represent ballplayers wearing protective gear—barred helmets, knee guards, and arm protectors—and each holds a small ball in his hand. Next to some are glyphs as yet undeciphered. In front of the platform and to the north is a partially reconstructed ballcourt similar in size and shape to the one at Monte Albán. We know from these figures that the ballgame was played here in Preclassic times; but the game was probably different from the one played in Postclassic times as described by the Spaniards or the Classic period game depicted on Maya vases because of differing court shape and goal placement.

A very steep hill, Cerro Dainzú, rises about 800 feet above the building that displays the incised figures. Originally, construction covered its face, and five additional carved figures adorned the cliff face near the top.

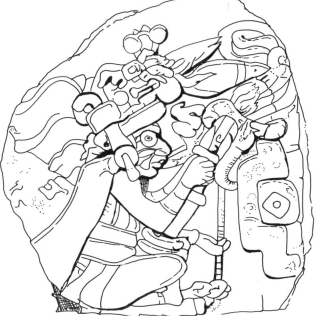

The base of a huge Monte Albán II–style platform was faced with some fifty boulders carved with figures, most of them ballplayers. Pictured is a seated deity wearing an elaborate headdress. (Drawing by Ethne Barnes).

Opposite, above: Late Preclassic Dainzú, seen here from the northwest, was closely tied to the Zapotec culture of Monte Albán. Below: Dainzú was built against a mountain in the valley a dozen miles southeast of modern Oaxaca. Its carvings may indicate an Olmec connection.

Above: The small excavated portion of Lambityeco (late Classic or early Postclassic) sits near the highway about 18 miles southeast of Oaxaca. Beneath the protective coverings placed there by the archaeologists are some fine sculptures. Left: Temple facade at Lambityeco. Below: Stucco head of the Zapotec rain deity, Cocijo.

CHAPTER THREE

Lowland Maya

Geographically, the territory occupied by the ancient Maya can be divided into three general zones: the Pacific Coast and Guatemala highlands, the lowlands (including Chiapas, Mexico, and Belize), and the Yucatán Peninsula of Mexico. The Maya lowlands form a crescent to the north and east of the mountains from Copán (east of Guatemala City) to Comalcalco on the coast of the Gulf of Mexico (near Villahermosa). Maya sites we discuss in this region include Copán; Quiriguá on the Motagua River of southeastern Guatemala; and Tikal, Río Azul, Seibal, and Uaxactun in the rain forest of the Petén. Other lowland sites include Xunantunich just east over the border in Belize, and Yaxchilán and Palenque near the Usumacinta River to the north and west in Chiapas, which we cover in chapters four and five.

Preclassic lowland Maya cultural attributes seem to have been derived primarily from roots in Belize with some borrowing from the ancient Olmecs through the cultural intermediary of Kaminaljuyú in the Guatemala highlands and the Teotihuacanos from the Valley of Mexico.

By about A.D. 50, Maya pyramid-plaza architecture, ballcourts, pyramid tombs, carved stone stelae, corbelled vaults, and polychrome pottery had become staples of lowland Maya culture. Central to the flourishing of the Maya civilization was the universality of language. Maya Indians from Dzibilchaltún near the north coast of Yucatán to Copán in Honduras spoke, and later wrote, a mutually understandable language.

Previously many scholars thought the impetus for

Maya Historical Stages	
Preclassic	
Early	2500–1000 B.C.
Middle	1000–300 B.C.
Late	300 B.C.–A.D. 250
Classic	A.D. 250–900
Postclassic	A.D. 900–1540

cultural development in the Classic stage emanated from non-Maya Mesoamerican peoples such as the Olmecs and the people of Teotihuacán. Recent discoveries at the Belize sites of Cerros and Cuello argue for indigenous development of Maya culture by Maya people beginning in early Preclassic times and continuing into the Classic stage. To this core many borrowed cultural attributes may have been added. From the Olmecs came the concept of a strong leader or king, the bloodletting ceremony, the ballgame, the bar-and-dot numeration system, and the ancestral Maya language (although many anthropologists argue the language came from Belize). Teotihuacán, in the Valley of Mexico, contributed military and commercial assistance that enabled lowland regional states such as Tikal to survive and flourish in Classic times while others (such as El Mirador, the huge Preclassic city north of Tikal on the border between Guatemala and Mexico), were abandoned by the end of the Preclassic.

The Golden Age of the Maya refers to the Classic

stage from A.D. 250 to 900. During Classic times the Maya lowlands contained numerous city-states. Adams suggests there may have been twelve to sixteen, each more or less independent of the other, yet bound together by a similar language and culture and often ruled by royal families who were interrelated by blood or marriage. Adams now believes that Teotihuacán became actively involved with the developing Maya city-states in the lowlands beginning in the middle A.D. 300s.

The organization of Maya society may have resembled European medieval feudalism to the extent that nobles owned or controlled the land that produced the food. These elite families, born to power, owed allegiance to the king and in turn received allegiance from the people who worked the land. Commerce, trade, building, and the production of goods probably was also controlled by the noble families. We know from the painted vessels found in graves depicting Maya lords and ladies, nobles, captives, slaves, and servants that the elite of the Maya lived sumptuous lives. Their standard of living compared favorably with any in the world at that time.

Maya lords were obsessed with ceremonial ritual and with warfare, especially the capture, humiliation, torture, and sacrifice of lords from other cities. They regularly inflicted upon themselves painful bloodletting rituals by cutting or piercing their ears, cheeks, tongues, and male genitals. The lords performed these rituals in the belief that their sacrifice would benefit all the people by appeasing the gods. Pottery vases portray the enema ritual—the ingestion of hallucinogenic or intoxicating fluids—to enable communication with deities. Even the ballgame involved the beheading of players. The Maya lords also believed if the gods were propitiated by properly performed ceremonies, death could be overcome and immortality achieved.

The cities contained streets and causeways, reservoirs, administrative buildings, palaces, huge rubble-filled and stone-faced pyramids topped with temples, and buildings with great plazas. Religious ceremonies were combined with regular market activities. Trade prospered between Maya cities and non-Maya regions especially in highland Mexico. Some cities were connected by surfaced roads. Scholars suggest the average Maya Indian expended about one-third of his time building public works.

The Maya were the only Precolumbian New World people to develop a full-fledged system of writing capable of expressing a broad spectrum of abstract thoughts. Between 200 B.C. and A.D. 150 most of the peoples in southern Mesoamerica employed basically the same calendric system. The Long Count system started from a fixed date beginning in 3114 B.C. and utilized a vigesimal system (by 20 instead of by 10 as we do) that was expressed in writing by bars and dots (a dot was equal to 1, a bar was equal to 5, and a shell was equal to 0). The Maya came nearly as close to calculating the number of days in a solar year as modern science has. The Maya astronomers could predict eclipses of the sun, and they knew the planet Venus was both a morning and evening star. (They envisioned Venus as the evening star pushing the sun into the underworld and as the morning star pulling it up.) Their monuments depicted calculations of supernatural events (like the birth of gods) that are either millions of years in the past or in the future.

Maya hieroglyphic writing appears on stelae, on altars, on walls and lintels of public buildings, and in the illuminated manuscripts called codices, a few of which survived the religious zeal of the Spaniards to destroy anything believed to be heathen. Many of the glyphs can now be translated. The hieroglyphs on stelae and public buildings generally recorded events in the life of the king and connected him with his ancestors, both actual and mythical.

Beginning around 10.0.0.0.0 in the Maya Long Count (equivalent to A.D. 830), the Classic Maya civilization of the southern lowlands began to fade. Warriors from the Puuc region are known to have raided Seibal, Quiriguá, and parts of Belize about this time. The final contributing factor probably was pressure from peoples outside the area, particularly the Maya from northern Yucatán, who raided the cities and cut the trade routes, destroying Maya city-states already weakened by overpopulation, overexpansion, and a failure of leadership.

Many died; others migrated to the north into Yucatán or into the Guatemala highlands. Some remained in the lowlands living as self-sufficient slash-and-burn farmers without the trappings of civilization. Postclassic Maya civilization continued, especially in the north where invading Mexicanized groups conquered Chichén Itzá, introducing highland Mexican architectural features, art, and the worship of Quetzalcoatl (Kukulcán in Maya) and other Mexican gods. Metallurgy, the manufacture of the distinctive plumbate pottery, and the use of turquoise became important features.

Discoveries made during the 1970s and 1980s have changed our perception of the Postclassic Maya. Recent archaeological research at Flores, Tayasal, and Topoxte in Guatemala; at Santa Rita Corozal, Altún Ha, and Lamanai in Belize; and at Tulum, Tancah, and Cozumel on the east coast of Yucatán indicates that these Postclassic Maya sites shared a common cultural base while maintaining great individual differences in artifacts, architecture, and urban planning. In the Petén during Postclassic times the island cities of Topoxte in Lake Yaxhá were fortified towns. Nearby Tayasal, on Lake Petén Itzá, was not conquered by the Spaniards until 1697.

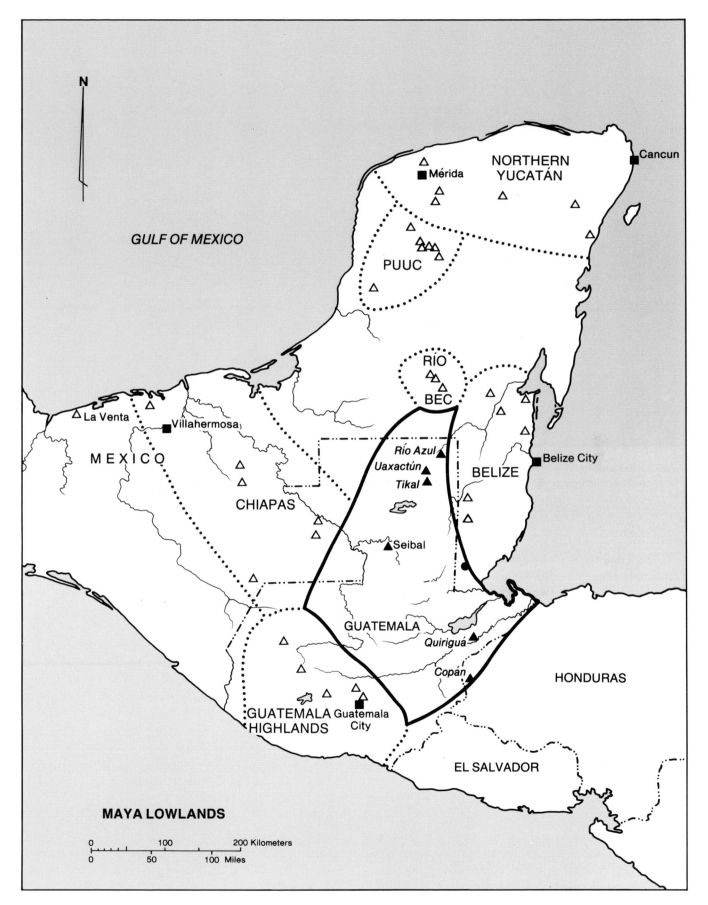

N

GULF OF MEXICO

NORTHERN YUCATÁN

■ Cancun

△
■ Mérida
△   △
△
△
△   △
△△△△
△
PUUC
△

RÍO
△△
△
BEC
△   △
△

La Venta △
△ Villahermosa

M E X I C O

Río Azul ▲
Uaxactún ▲
Tikal ▲

BELIZE

△
△   ■ Belize City

△
CHIAPAS

△
△   ▲ *Seibal*

△
△

GUATEMALA

Quiriguá ▲

HONDURAS

△   *Copán* ▲

GUATEMALA
HIGHLANDS

△
△
△   ■ Guatemala
City

EL SALVADOR

MAYA LOWLANDS

0   100   200 Kilometers
0   50   100 Miles

*The lowland Maya occupied the region north of the Sierra Madre mountain chain
from the Gulf Coast near Villahermosa, Mexico, to northwestern Honduras. The
outlined region includes the major Maya lowland Guatemala cities, plus Copán in
Honduras.*

Tikal, a jewel among Maya ruins, nestles in the rain forest of the Guatemala Petén.
The central portion of this great Classic Maya city has been restored.

TIKAL

The Tikal ruins are located in the Petén of northern Guatemala about 60 miles west of the Belize border, 40 miles by road northeast of Flores, and about 190 air miles north of Guatemala City. At Santa Elena, on the south shore across from the island town of Flores, the government of Guatemala has constructed a new jet airport to serve visitors to Tikal. In 1956, the University Museum of the University of Pennsylvania began a program of restoration and study at Tikal. The project continued for thirteen seasons, and the Guatemala government took over and continued restoration in 1969. Tikal, one of the major archaeological sites in the world, should be visited by every aficionado of Precolumbian culture.

During Classic times (beginning around A.D. 250) and before, Tikal stood out as a huge, gleaming, sparkling island of red pyramid-temples and white buildings and plazas in a sea of green forest and cultivated land. Tall temples crowned with roof combs displaying gigantic sculptures of rulers and gods jutted up toward the sky from the plazas. Paved streets crisscrossed the city, reservoirs of water dotted its expanse, and numerous stelae commemorated important events. In the center of the city spread a huge market. Smoke from burning copal on the temple stairways joined the smoke from hundreds of cooking fires, wafting upward to disappear in the blue sky. Stone palaces provided residences for the nobles. Merchants, warriors, artisans, and farmers lived in and around the city.

Only the partially restored temple-pyramids of Tikal now rise above the trees of the Petén rain forest. The Great Plaza, enclosed on the east by the Temple of the Giant Jaguar (Temple I) and on the west by the Temple of the Masks (Temple II), both constructed by the ruler Ah Cacaw in the late Maya Classic (ca. A.D. 700), now marks the focal point of restored Tikal. Toward the west rises the Temple of the Jaguar Priest (Temple III), the last of the pyramid-temples constructed at Tikal, built during the reign of Chitam (ca. A.D. 810). To the far west is the gigantic Temple IV built by Ruler B (ca. A.D. 750). Just south of the Great Plaza may be seen the unexcavated Temple V and further to the southeast the Temple of the Inscriptions (Temple VI), constructed by Ruler B and reworked by Chitam. The North Acropolis adjoins the Great Plaza on the north with the Central Acropolis on the south. More than 3,000 structures and 200 stone monuments lie hidden under the canopy of the rain forest.

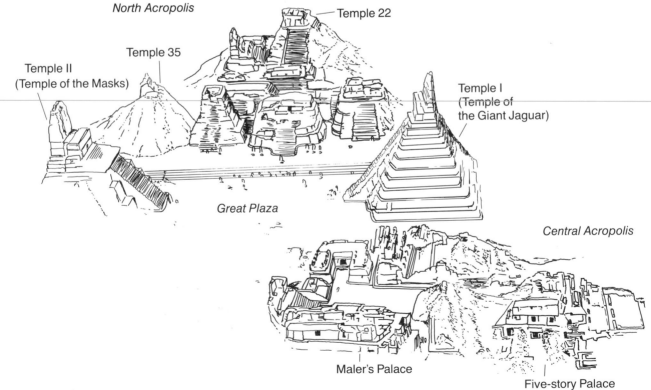

North Acropolis

Temple 22

Temple 35

Temple II
(Temple of the Masks)

Temple I
(Temple of
the Giant Jaguar)

Great Plaza

Central Acropolis

Maler's Palace

Five-story Palace

*The Great Plaza at Tikal is bounded by Temples I and II on the east and west, the
North Acropolis, and the Central Acropolis. The construction here represents Tikal
at the zenith of the Maya Classic.*

Opposite, above: Temple I (on the right) towers above the Great Plaza across from Temple II. Both temples were erected during the reign of Ah Cacaw around A.D. 700. On the floor of the plaza at the entrance to the North Acropolis are a row of stelae, some placed by the Classic Maya, others reset in Postclassic times. The North Acropolis, the construction of which continued for 1,000 years, consisted of temple-crowned pyramids built to serve as royal tombs or as temples dedicated to royal ancestors. The earliest construction dates from about 200 B.C. the acropolis contains about 100 structures. Below: The Palace (Central Acropolis) to the right of Temple I covers about 4 acres and contained six courts and many multistoried buildings. It was used as the residence for kings, nobles, and high priests, and it also probably was the center of administration for the city. This page: The Temple of the Giant Jaguar is one of the hallmarks—practically a logo—of modern Guatemala. Beneath the pyramid was the tomb of Ah Cacaw, probably Tikal's greatest king. In the late afternoon when the sun strikes the roof comb, the massive outline of Ah Cacaw can be seen sitting tailor-fashion on his throne.

Left: Stela 9, displaying Tikal's ruler Kan Chitam (Kan Boar) within a frame, contains the date 9.2.0.0.0 (A.D. 475). Above right: Stela 16, a monument to King Ah Cacaw, was erected to celebrate a 20-year period (katun) ending in A.D. 711. The glyphs carved to commemorate the event have been translated by Linda Schele on page 94.

In its golden age during the late Classic, Tikal may have housed more than 50,000 people. The city's beginnings can be traced back beyond 300 B.C. and it continued to be an important city until nearly A.D. 900 when, like the other Classic centers of the Maya lowlands, it was abandoned. Recent research by Clemency

Coggins, Christopher Jones, and others has identified and placed in chronological context more than twenty Tikal rulers. Scroll Ahau Jaguar is the earliest ruler as yet identified and may have ruled from around A.D. 292. Stormy Sky, who was probably the eleventh king of Tikal (A.D. 426–457), is the most notable of the early rulers. Ah Cacaw (Ah Cacao Caan Chac) was the great builder of later Classic times (682–734) who was responsible for the restored center of Tikal visible today. The last recorded king of Tikal is the Stela 11 Ruler (ca. A.D. 869).

Tikal became one of the great cities of the Maya. Although not as large as Teotihuacán in the Mexican highlands, it was probably the largest of the Maya cities during Classic times. Situated near the center of the Maya lowlands in a portage area between the east-west rivers from the Caribbean coast and the Pasión and Usumacinta River regions, it functioned as a trade center well-supplied with food produced from nearby raised fields. R.E.W. Adams, who has recently been excavating the newly discovered great site of Río Azul near the

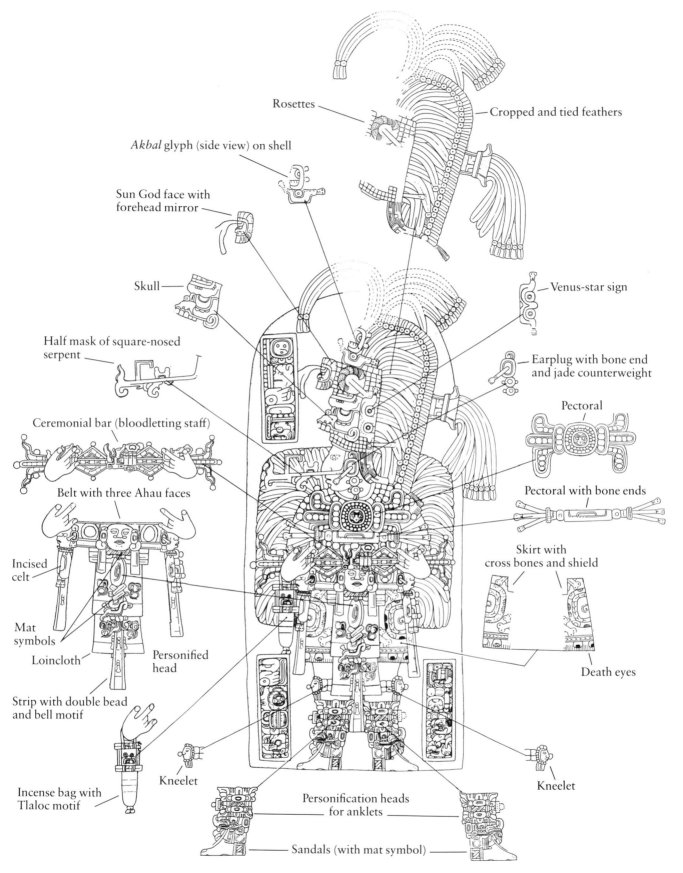

Rosettes

Cropped and tied feathers

Akbal glyph (side view) on shell

Sun God face with forehead mirror

Venus-star sign

Skull

Earplug with bone end and jade counterweight

Half mask of square-nosed serpent

Pectoral

Ceremonial bar (bloodletting staff)

Pectoral with bone ends

Belt with three Ahau faces

Skirt with cross bones and shield

Incised celt

Mat symbols

Death eyes

Loincloth

Personified head

Strip with double bead and bell motif

Incense bag with Tlaloc motif

Kneelet

Kneelet

Personification heads for anklets

Sandals (with mat symbol)

Stela 16, Tikal. Iconography interpreted by Linda Schele. Drawing by W. R. Coe.

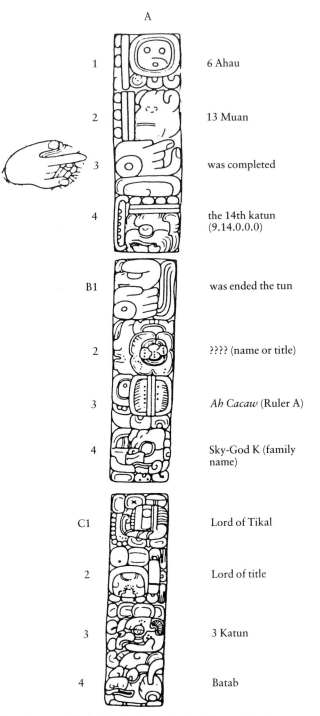

A 1	6 Ahau
2	13 Muan
3	was completed
4	the 14th katun (9.14.0.0.0)
B1	was ended the tun
2	???? (name or title)
3	*Ah Cacaw* (Ruler A)
4	Sky-God K (family name)
C1	Lord of Tikal
2	Lord of title
3	3 Katun
4	Batab

Paraphrase of Stela 16 glyphs, stela dated December 5, A.D. 711. (Drawing by W. R. Coe, Linda Schele, Maya Hieroglyphic Writing Workshop*).*

Guatemala-Mexico-Belize border, concludes that Río Azul was established by Stormy Sky as an outpost of Tikal. He also suggests that Tikal's alliance with Teotihuacán enabled it to become the dominant city in the region during the early Classic; that dominance continued through Classic times.

The North Acropolis consisted of temple-crowned pyramids built to serve as royal tombs or as temples dedicated to royal ancestors. They were built either by the lord himself during his lifetime or by his progeny or successors in veneration of the deceased lord; the deceased were assumed to have conquered death, thus becoming deities to be worshiped by the living lords. In all, the North Acropolis contains portions of as many as 100 structures, the earliest of which dates from around 200 B.C. Tombs for Jaguar Paw (Temple 26), Stormy Sky (Temple 33), and Curl Nose (Temple 34) have been found in this acropolis.

The Palace area (Central Acropolis) lies just to the south of the Great Plaza. This late Classic complex consisted of range-type buildings (some with several stories) surrounding six courts on various levels. These buildings were used by the upper echelon of Maya society for residences and for running the government. The east end of the central Acropolis (Courts 4 and 6) contained a five-story palace thought to have been used by the high priests and the Great Eastern Court Palace complex constructed before A.D. 600 and continually occupied as a lord's residence until nearly A.D. 900.

In celebration of the 9.17.0.0.0 (A.D. 771) katun ending, the rulers of Tikal constructed Twin-Pyramid Complex Q (there were nine such complexes of flat-topped pyramids without temples at Tikal). A katun (20 tuns) was 7,200 days, or twenty 360-day years, the passage of which was generally celebrated by the construction of a pyramid and by self-induced bloodletting by the ruler.

Restoration and stabilization of the Tikal ruins continue under the direction of the government of Guatemala.

QUIRIGUÁ

The ruins of Quiriguá occupy a small island of primeval forest of giant ceibas, mahoganies, and cohune palms surrounded by a sea of banana plants on the Motagua River about 135 miles northeast of Guatemala City. In 1910, the United Fruit Company set aside what is now the Quiriguá Park. Some restoration of the ruins was accomplished in the late nineteenth century by A. P. Maudslay, and from time to time between 1915 and 1934, S. G. Morley worked there. Recent restoration has been conducted by the University Museum of the University of Pennsylvania.

The visible ruins were built during a period of about 300 years, from A.D. 550 to 850. Robert J. Sharer has identified five of the rulers: Cauac Sky, Sky Xul, Imix Dog, Scroll Sky, and Jade Sky. Cauac Sky became king in A.D. 724 and the latest known ruler was Jade Sky, who acceded to the throne in A.D. 805. Huge, beautifully carved stone stelae in the Great Plaza memorialize Cauac Sky who reigned for sixty years. Stela E bears the image of Lord Cauac Sky and was erected to celebrate the katun ending 9.17.0.0.0 (A.D. 771). This stela weighs

Great Plaza of Quiriguá from south to north with Stela J, dated 9.16.5.0.0
(A.D. 756), in the foreground.

about 65 tons, with a shaft length of 35 feet, surpassing the height of all other stelae at Quiriguá and probably all others erected by the Maya. Next to Stela E stands Stela F, erected ten years earlier in A.D. 761, which shows Cauac Sky's accession to the throne in 724. Stela D typifies Cauac Sky's magnificent monuments with full-figure glyphs along its sides that date the stela to the hotun (half katun) ending 9.16.15.0.0 7 Ahau 18 Pop (A.D. 766).

Zoomorph P, the Great Turtle, is Quiriguá's most famous monument. This huge boulder was delicately carved on all its sides and top in A.D. 795 under commission from either Sky Xul or Imix Dog. The ruler's figure appears on the north face, the Cauac Monster's eye on the east side, and the south face portrays some monster, either a Skeletal Sun Monster or Principal Bird Deity.

The acropolis, a residential complex for the rulers of Quiriguá, was entered by a massive east-west stairway from the ballcourt plaza. The ruins of Jade Sky's palace sit at the lower end of the plaza at the top of the stairway, and the much earlier palace of Cauac Sky appears next to it.

Quiriguá is a Classic Maya site on the Motagua River in Guatemala. Monuments have been found indicating early occupation—around A.D. 475–495. The visible ruins cover a period from A.D. 550 to 850. The Quiriguá Park is surrounded by cultivation, mostly banana plants.

Opposite: Plan of Quiriguá.

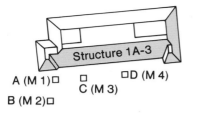

Structure 1A-3

A (M 1) □   □   □ D (M 4)

C (M 3)

B (M 2) □

N

E (M 5) □   □ F (M 6)

□ G (M 7)

GREAT PLAZA

□ H (M 8)

□ I (M 9)

J (M 10) □   □ K (M 11)

Ballcourt Plaza   M (M 13)
○
○
N (M 14)

○ O (M 15)

Palace 1B 5)

P (M 16) ○ ○
○   O Altar (M 23)

ACROPOLIS

Residential Structures

QUIRIGUA

Cauac Sky Palace

Jade Sky Palace

0   50   100 Meters
0   150   300 Feet

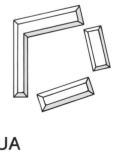

Above left: Stela E (Monument 5) bears the carved image of Quiriguá's great king, Cauac Sky, who ruled for 60 years beginning in A.D. 724. The stela weighs 65 tons and has a shaft length of 35 feet; it is probably the tallest ever erected by the Maya. Above right: Stela C (A.D. 775) was one of the last stelae erected by Ruler Cauac Sky. The stela contains the Quiriguá emblem glyph and Cauac Sky's name glyph. Below right, left to right: Quiriguá emblem glyph, Stela C 6, and Cauac Sky's name glyph, Stela C.

Right: Stela I at Quiriguá was erected in A.D. 800, near the end of the Maya Classic, and may indicate the accession of Ruler Scroll Sky. Below: The carved boulder designated Zoomorph B (Monument 2) probably depicts Ruler Cauac Sky emerging from a celestial monster carved with crossed bands in its eyes.

Zoomorph P (Monument 16), the Great Turtle, dated A.D. 795, is Quiriguá's most famous monument. This huge boulder is intricately carved on all sides. The south face here shown depicts either a Serpent Bird or a Skeletal Sun Monster. Robert Sharer suggests it was carved either to mark the end of the reign of Sky Xul or the accession of Imix Dog.

Quiriguá continued to flourish after many other Classic Maya sites were abandoned, persisting after 10.0.0.0.0 (A.D. 830), until at least A.D. 850. Some evidence for Postclassic use of the city include copper items, green obsidian, a chacmool sculpture of the Tula-Toltec type, and Postclassic plumbate pottery with a lead-like glaze finish. It has been suggested that a massive earthquake caused the ultimate demise of Quiriguá; but Sharer suggests the downfall may have been the result of a military raid by the northern Maya from the Yucatán.

COPÁN

Copán marks the southeasternmost principal Maya Classic city. It is situated in a mountain valley on the western edge of Honduras, not more than 4 or 5 miles from the Guatemala border and near the picturesque Spanish colonial town now called Ruinas de Copán. Don Diego Garcia de Palacio wrote to Philip II of Spain in 1576:

> Near here in Copán, the first town within the province of Honduras, on the road to the city of San Pedro, we came across certain ruins and remains of what seems to have been a great civilization. There are structures built with such skill and splendor that it seems that they could not have been built by the natives of that province. They are located on the banks of a beautiful river in an extensive and well-chosen plain.

The Copán Valley runs east-west for about 8 miles, is 1.5 miles wide, and is cut by the Copán River flowing northwest into the Motagua River in Guatemala. The valley lies about 2,000 feet above sea level and is ringed

Copán, Honduras, viewed from the north, shows the Great Plaza, the ballcourt, and the Copán River in the background. The excavated ruins cover about 40 acres and contain an acropolis and five plazas. Most of the buildings and monuments were erected during late Classic times between A.D. 600 and 800.

by tree-covered mountains that rise another 1,000 feet above the valley floor. The climate is warm and dry in the winter and warm and rainy in the summer. Copán lies in the mountains above the jungles and rain forests.

In recent years the entire Copán Valley has been carefully studied so that it is now known where the ancient people lived, how they lived, when they moved, and where. The excavations indicate some 20,000 people were living around the central core of the city in Classic times.

*This portion of Copán was a true ceremonial center since no palaces or other
residential units were included here. The acropolis was virtually sealed off from the
lower plaza and was probably reserved for the elite.*

The excavated ruins cover about 40 acres and consist of the acropolis and five plazas. The visible buildings, erected during the late Classic between A.D. 600 and 800, are surrounded by complexes of some 3,500 mounds where elite and commoner families lived. Two urban enclaves, El Bosque and Las Sepulturas, residences of the elite, have been identified lying outside the royal city. A causeway connected Las Sepulturas with the Main Group. The core of Copán was ceremonial. In ancient times, Copán's acropolis was virtually sealed off from the courts and plazas to the north. The only access was through the Temple of the Inscriptions or by way of the Hieroglyphic Stairway, reserving it for use by the elite. The glyphic record shows Mah K'ina Yax K'uk' Mo', Great Sun Lord Quetzal Macaw, was the earliest verified Copán ruler. There is a reference to him on a monument bearing the date, December 11, 435. Later kings mention being in his lineage. The inscriptions indicate seventeen kings reigned at Copán, but only about a dozen have been identified. The clearest record begins with Moon Jaguar, Ruler 10, who became king in 553,

followed by Butz Chan, Smoke Imix (628 to 695) who fostered Copán's first great period of building, 18 Rabbit, Smoke Monkey, Smoke Shell, Yax Pac, and the seventeenth and last known ruler, U Cit Tok', who acceded late in Maya Classic times, A.D. 822.

Copán's best known ruler, 18 Rabbit, met an unhappy fate when Quiriguá's King Cauac Sky captured him on May 3, 738. He was later sacrificed. Copán's Great Plaza is studded with stelae erected by 18 Rabbit. Linda Schele's recent work at Copán has shown that the acropolis was known as Macaw Mountain. Its showpiece, the Temple of Meditation (Structure 22) with its strikingly modern-looking stone sculpture surrounding the inner door, was built by 18 Rabbit.

Copán's masterpiece, the Hieroglyphic Stairway leading up from the plaza to the acropolis, was constructed during the reign of Smoke Shell, and his likeness appeared on the top. In the middle appeared 18 Rabbit. Although one of the great architectural monuments in the world, the stairway lost its value as a historical document because most of the glyph steps, which

Bat (T 756)	Ben Ich Prefix (T 168)	Cauac (T 528)	Copán Emblem Glyph

were found in modern times in a pile at the bottom, have been replaced at random by the restorers. The stairway, now being reconstructed displays a recitation of the names of the rulers' progenitors, actual and mythological, in much the same way as do the glyph panels in the Temple of the Inscriptions at Palenque. Some 1,250 glyphs incorporated in the stairway reveal the dynastic history of Copán to the year 755. Prior to this reconstruction, thirty dates had been deciphered extending for 200 years from A.D. 544 to 744. Beneath the stairway a cache planted by 18 Rabbit has been discovered containing jade figures, a shell, stingray spines, and eccentric flints. Traces of blood were found on the shell, indicating it probably was used for ritual bloodletting. Even further behind the stairway, archaeologists also found a tomb containing the remains of a sacrificial victim and a noble scribe thought to have been the son

Above: The flat-topped Pyramid 4 was remodeled for the last time in A.D. 731 and divides the Great Plaza and the Central Court at Copán. In the center sits the ballcourt, behind which rises the famous Hieroglyphic Stairway. Below: Glyphs that make up the Copán emblem glyph.

of Smoke Imix. Interred with the deceased were numerous jade ornaments.

Copán's visible structures are primarily late Classic. Although royal Copán died in the early 800s, people continued to live in the valley until A.D. 1200. In earlier times, Preclassic farmers settled in the region as early as 1000 B.C. Luxury goods found in Preclassic burials indicate early Olmec connections and trade with the Valley of Guatemala as early as 900 B.C. Thus Precolumbian Copanos have lived in the valley, more or less continuously for at least 2000 years.

Above: The Hieroglyphic Stairway was made up of more than 2,500 glyph blocks, but the stairway collapsed in ancient times and the blocks were replaced at random, making reading the text extremely difficult. The stairway is now being rebuilt correctly. Below: The Ballcourt was rebuilt at least three times. Reconstruction by Copán's most famous ruler, 18 Rabbit, took place around A.D. 700. The last renovation date was 9.17.4.0.0 (A.D. 775), during the reign of Yax Pac.

Copán's Great Plaza, 18 Rabbit's showcase, contained eight stelae and several altars, most of which were erected by 18 Rabbit during late Classic times. We may assume that this plaza, replete with stelae and altars, was utilized for public ceremonies.

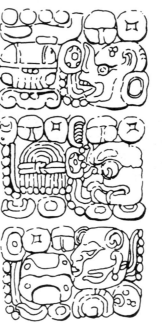

Copán

Tikal

Palenque

Above: In the background are Stelae B and 4, which were dedicated to 18 Rabbit in A.D. 731. Stela C (foreground) is the subject of scholarly debate. Linda Schele feels it was erected around A.D. 731 by 18 Rabbit; Claude Baudez suggests A.D. 782. These stelae are extraordinary because they feature sculpture in the round. Left: Stela A was erected by 18 Rabbit in A.D. 731. The large head was probably designed to emphasize the ruler's face. On the side of Stela A are the emblem glyphs of Copán, Tikal, and Palenque.

The bicephalic (two-headed) turtle has claws like a jaguar, one head with fangs, and the other with a serrated row of teeth. In the background stands Stela B.

A portion of the Copán ruins were destroyed by the flow of the Copán River before it was rechanneled in modern times. The southeastern portion of the Copán ruins show the erosion and the recently excavated Temple 18 that may have been the funerary monument of Yax Pac (Rising Sun).

Left: This sculpted head of the Maize God from Copán in the collections of the British Museum of Mankind provides a superb example of the Copán art style of total three-dimensional representation. The graceful lines of this figure rival any classic Greek sculpture. Top: Altar G, a double-headed serpent, may have been carved as late as A.D. 800. Right: God N, known as the Old Man of Copán.

CHAPTER FOUR

Belize Maya

Recent discoveries indicate that the region encompassed by modern-day Belize (formerly British Honduras) was an important cradle of Classic Maya culture. Discoveries by Richard S. MacNeish and others indicate the Maya forebears had settled along the coast of Belize as early as 4200 B.C., first as fishermen, and then as sedentary farmers of corn, beans, and squash.

At Cuello, in northern Belize, excavations by Norman Hammond demonstrate continuous occupation beginning about 2500 B.C. and extending to at least 450 B.C. These people, whose culture was basic Maya, were probably the earliest known direct antecedents of the Classic Maya. By the middle Preclassic (1000 B.C.), pyramid-plaza ceremonial architecture, Maya house design, food staples, pottery, and government by the elite were well established at Cuello.

At Cerros, also in northern Belize on the shallow south side of Bahia Chetumal, David Freidel and his associates have shown that Maya Preclassic culture was flourishing between 50 B.C. and A.D. 100. Cerros was a trading center dealing in chert tools, salt, obsidian, and jade. The city center included ballcourts, vaulted pyramid tombs, stelae demonstrating a ruling elite, and pyramid-plaza ceremonial structures.

For a long time archaeologists had traced Maya culture from Olmec beginnings in the Gulf Coast region around San Lorenzo and La Venta (1200–400 B.C.), through Izapa on the Pacific coast near modern Tapachula, Mexico, and then to the Guatemala highland city of Kaminaljuyú. Undoubtedly, many Classic Maya cultural characteristics are traceable to the Olmec: the stelae cult, bloodletting, and the bar-and-dot numeration system. But now we know that many Classic Maya characteristics originated in Belize: masonry buildings, stone tools, perhaps language, pyramid-plaza ceremonial construction, an elite society, and human sacrifice.

Altún Ha, in central Belize, had a long history extending from the Preclassic—as early as 200 B.C.—through the Classic. Construction probably stopped around A.D. 800, but occupation continued well into the Postclassic. It is unlikely that Altún Ha was continuously occupied for the entire 1,500 years from 200 B.C. to the A.D. 1300s because there is no evidence of the Maya living there during the A.D. 1000s and 1100s.

We now know Belize constituted an important component within the Classic lowland Maya region. Caracol, in the jungles of the Maya Mountains in western Belize, was a large city-state covering an area of some 100 square miles with an estimated population of 40,000. The inscriptions tell us that Caracol at one time conquered mighty Tikal, 60 miles to the northwest. The site of Xunantunich near the border village of Benque Viejo del Carmen on the tortuous road between Guatemala and Belize is a mostly Classic Maya ruin. It boasts a spectacular, huge, restored stucco mask facade along the east side of El Castillo, the principal pyramid of the city.

Kohunlich in Quintana Roo, Mexico, west of the Mexican city, Chetumal, is noted for its magnificent stucco masks of the Sun God. The city is considered to be very late Preclassic, flourishing during the first two or three centuries A.D., making it contemporaneous with Cerros and El Mirador, although some authorities place the city and the masks in early Classic times. The ruins focus on a so-called Ceremonial Plaza surrounded by four building groups. On the north side of the plaza is a large structure—almost an acropolis—crowned by palaces.

The Maya built a west-facing pyramid on a small natural hill just to the east of the city's center. Flanking the stairway on each side are a series of marvelously preserved, large human-like stucco masks of the Sun God—sculpture unsurpassed anywhere in Mayaland. The masks are covered by thatched roofing placed there to protect them from erosion.

ALTÚN HA

In 1964, the Royal Ontario Museum of Toronto began to excavate and restore the beautiful tropical Maya ruin at Altún Ha; work continued through 1970. The excavations revealed a fairly extensive settlement as early as 200 B.C. with construction beginning at the northern plaza (Plaza A) by early in the Christian Era. By A.D. 150–200 building was underway in the southern plaza (Plaza B). Only the ceremonial and elite residential section of the city has been restored. In the 240 acres of dense ruins, the Ontario team identified more than 275 structures, and in the adjoining area of 365 acres, they found 250 mounds and numerous house floors.

David M. Pendergast, who prepared a guidebook to Altún Ha (1976), suggests the Maya believed that a temple had a sort of life span. A temple was used for a period of time and then remodeled; the old temple-pyramid was covered with a new structure, much larger than its predecessor. Archaeologists are thus able to observe changes in construction over the centuries. The sequence of rebuilding at Altún Ha seemed to roughly follow a 50-year cycle (approximating the 52-year Mayan calendar cycle) until about A.D. 800; but Altún Ha was apparently occupied throughout the Postclassic even though there was no significant construction after Classic times. Little is known about the rulers of Altún Ha because no carved stone monuments have yet been found to give the names of the kings and the dates of their reigns. Pendergast speculates that final collapse of the city may have been brought about by a violent peasant revolt. He found no evidence of military invasion, famine, or pestilence contributing to the demise of the Classic government.

The excavated plazas give the visitor the feeling of being in a lush green park surrounded by a tropical forest—Plaza A lies to the north and Plaza B to the south. Over the centuries the Maya rebuilt the base of the north plaza seven times, so the final plaster surface covered a prior fill about 6 feet thick. Construction of the temple-pyramids surrounding Plaza A began as early as the first century A.D. The Temple of the Green Tomb (A-1), so-called because of the presence of nearly three hundred jade artifacts found in a ruler's tomb there, stands on the west side of the plaza. It was rebuilt several times and achieved its final form about A.D. 500. This temple-pyramid was connected to residential structures to the south. On the east side of the plaza rises temple A-5 and to the north a large mass of rubble, designated A-6, is topped with a partially excavated range-type building more than 150 feet long.

The Temple of the Masonry Altars (B-4) dominates Plaza B from the east side. The frontal stairway and building made up of a series of vaulted rooms dates from about A.D. 650. Excavators removed some of the latest construction to stabilize the pyramid. In the course of excavation, seven tombs within the pyramid were revealed. Some had been looted in ancient times suggesting the possibility of violence or revolt against the rulers. Along the south border of Plaza B, the Maya erected residential buildings. The earliest platforms date about A.D. 150. The buildings of Plaza B in the form they now appear date from Classic times, about A.D. 600 and later.

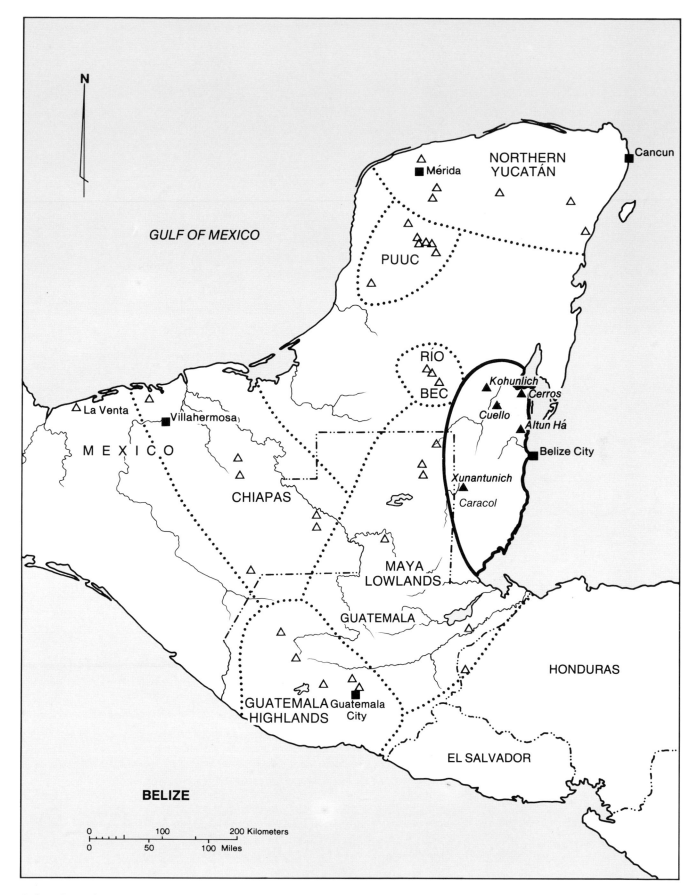

N

GULF OF MEXICO

NORTHERN YUCATÁN

△ ■ Mérida
△
△ △
△ ■ Cancun

PUUC
△△△△
△
△
△

RIO
△
△ BEC

Kohunlich ▲
▲ Cerros
Cuello ▲
Altun Há ▲
■ Belize City

La Venta △
■ Villahermosa

M E X I C O
△
△

CHIAPAS
△
△

△
△
Xunantunich ▲
Caracol

MAYA
LOWLANDS

GUATEMALA

HONDURAS

△
△
△

GUATEMALA
HIGHLANDS Guatemala
City ■
△

EL SALVADOR

BELIZE

0   100   200 Kilometers
0   50   100 Miles

*Belize, Central America, contains a full spectrum of Mesoamerican settlements:
along the coast, there is evidence of man as early as 10,000 B.C.; at Cuello,
occupation by early Maya peoples from 2500 B.C.; at Cerros a flourishing Preclassic
Maya city; and magnificent Classic cities at Altún Ha, Xunantunich, and Kohunlich.*

As a trading center for chert tools, salt, and obsidian on the coast in extreme northern Belize, Cerros was a prosperous Preclassic Maya city at the beginning of the Christian Era. It had canals, raised fields, and a seagoing canoe basin.

Above: Cuello, one of the earliest known Maya settlements, had pyramid-plaza ceremonial architecture and Maya house design by 1000 B.C. Below: From its beginnings about 200 B.C., Altún Ha was occupied well into Postclassic times, although there was little construction done after A.D. 800. Seen here is the city's ceremonial center.

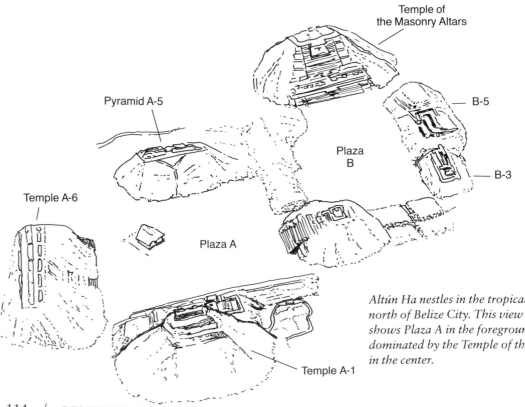

Temple of
the Masonry Altars

Pyramid A-5

Temple A-6

Plaza A

Plaza
B

B-5

B-3

Temple A-1

*Altún Ha nestles in the tropical forest about 30 miles
north of Belize City. This view from the northwest
shows Plaza A in the foreground and Plaza B,
dominated by the Temple of the Masonry Altars,
in the center.*

Above: On the east side of Plaza B at Altún Ha stands the Temple of the Masonry Altars (B-4), with foundation plat-forms built as early as A.D. 150. The temple as it now appears dates from about A.D. 650. Seven tombs were discovered during excavation, including the Sun God's tomb that contained a huge jade head of Kinich Ahau, the Maya Sun God. *Below: The partially restored Temple of the Green Tomb (more than three hundred jade objects were found in a tomb within the pyramid) sits on the west side of Plaza A. Its final form dates from around A.D. 500. Altún Ha's plazas were not sprinkled with stelae as were plazas in most other Classic Maya cities.*

Above: Terrace facade of the Temple of the Masonry Altars at Altún Ha. Below: These typical Maya corbelled arched buildings extended across the front of the Temple of the Masonry Altars.

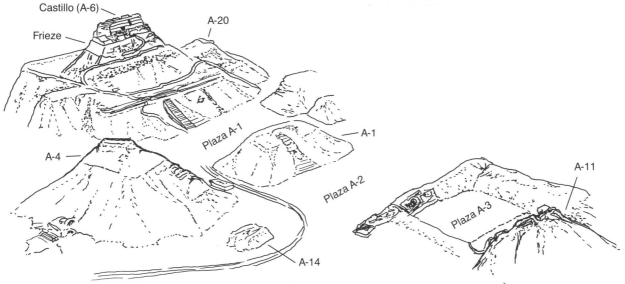

Castillo (A-6)

Frieze

A-20

A-4

Plaza A-1

A-1

Plaza A-2

A-14

Plaza A-3

A-11

Xunantunich, a Classic Maya ruin crowning a hill near the little village of Benque Viejo del Carmen, is shown from the northeast. In the background the Guatemala airport-of-entry—a short, rough, sod strip used to pasture livestock between landings—may be seen.

Above: Xunantunich crests a hill running from north to south. The huge El Castillo (A-6) lies at the south end of the ruin and faces Plaza A-I. A. H. Anderson completed uncovering the magnificent stucco frieze in the 1959–1960 season, and its restoration was done by Joseph O. Palacio. The Maya built over the frieze in a reconstruction of the pyramid, thus preserving it. Below: Restored mask of the Sun God, part of the stucco frieze on the Xunantunich El Castillo.

El Castillo at Xunantunich.

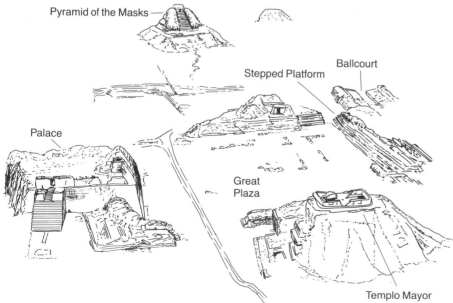

Pyramid of the Masks

Palace

Stepped Platform

Ballcourt

Great Plaza

Templo Mayor

Kohunlich (a corruption of Cohun Ridge), about 40 miles west of Chetumal, Mexico, is a late Preclassic Maya center. Reportedly the site was discovered by a Mexican farmer, or perhaps looters, in the late 1960s.

Above: In the foreground, Kohunlich's Pyramid of the Masks sits at the east end of two ceremonial plazas. Below: The Pyramid of the Masks, seen here from the south, rises in four sloping terraces with rounded corners toward a flat top where the temple stood. The sloping thatched roof, installed by the restorers of the site, acts as a protective shield for the beautifully preserved set of stucco masks that flank the broad west stairway.

The terrace facades on each side of the stairway mounting the Pyramid of the Masks (Kohunlich) are ornamented by carved stucco masks covering stone bases. The lower four, two on each side, present the Sun God, Kinich Ahau, in a strikingly humanized form.

The stucco masks that make up the four lower panels are some of the most refined and sensitive deity portrayals in all Meso-america. Each mask represents the same deity that has been identified as Kinich Ahau, the Sun God. Originally, each of the masks on the Pyramid of the Masks at Kohunlich had been painted in bright colors. Much of the red paint still adheres to the stucco surfaces.

CHAPTER FIVE

Maya Cities of Chiapas

Chiapas is Mexico's southeasternmost state bordering on Guatemala. The Usumacinta River forms the eastern boundary, carrying waters from several rivers that flow west and north out of the mountains of southern Chiapas and Guatemala and from the Petén rain forests. The Usumacinta flows through wild country between Guatemala and Mexico until it reaches the swampy flatland north of the mountains, and from there it wanders north toward the Gulf of Mexico. The Maya established several important cities along the river's path: Yaxchilán, Bonampak, Toniná, and Palenque in what is now modern Mexico, and Piedras Negras and Altar de Sacrificios in Guatemala. In the adjacent state of Tabasco, not far from the capital city of Villahermosa and near the sea, stood the westernmost Maya city of Comalcalco.

Palenque perches on the northern edge of the Sierra de Chiapas, where it shines as one of the brightest stars of Mayaland. With all its grandeur, Palenque was a late bloomer, becoming a city of consequence only from the middle A.D. 400s to about 800.

Yaxchilán's buildings and temples are built upon the jungle-covered hills that rise on the Mexican side of the Usumacinta River. Where the river makes an omega-shaped bend stands a beautiful Classic Maya city with exciting and well-preserved inscriptions. In ancient times the city rose from the river's edge in tier after tier of graceful roof-combed buildings and beautifully carved stelae, stone altars, and panels. The great Jaguar family of kings ruled Yaxchilán during late Classic times. The most feasible means of getting to Yaxchilán is by air-

plane; but a visit, although expensive, is immeasurably rewarding.

Bonampak, like its neighbor Yaxchilán just over the ridge to the east, can also best be reached by air. The airstrip is hemmed in by 100-foot-high ceiba trees. The first step in landing involves buzzing the nearby village and circling while the Indians drive the donkeys and goats off the strip. Because the tops of the ceiba trees tend to grow together, landing at Bonampak is like landing in the mouth of a tunnel. As at all mountain airstrips, you land uphill toward the mountain and take off downhill toward the valley. Bonampak's ruins adjoin the strip.

Bonampak, only a small Classic site, is famous for its magnificent murals depicting events in the lives of Maya nobility: the designation of a young lord as heir by his father, Chaan-muan, in A.D. 792; the torture and sacrifice of captives in connection with the heliacal rising of Venus; and preparations for the bloodletting ceremony by the lords.

Toniná is a small site located on terraces in a beautiful valley near the Chiapas village of Ocosingo, about 75 miles south on the road from Palenque to San Cristóbal de las Casas. The site is renowned for its record of the capture and sacrifice of Kan Xul, king of Palenque. A stela erected at Toniná indicates his capture in A.D. 711. The Palenque record reveals that his successor, Xoc, did not accede to the throne of Palenque until A.D. 720, suggesting Kan Xul may have been held hostage for those years. It was a common practice among the Maya to capture, hold, and torture for years, and finally ex-

125

ecute rulers from other cities. Toniná is also renowned for the discovery there of one of the latest known Initial Series stelae; bearing the date 10.4.0.0.0 (A.D. 909), the stela shows that Toniná was occupied as a Classic city longer than its neighbors.

Chinkultic occupies a spectacular mountain setting about 75 miles south of San Cristóbal de las Casas in the highlands of southeast Mexico along the Pan-American Highway. The ancient Greeks would have approved of the mountain location. Chinkultic exhibits characteristics of both Classic Maya lowland and Guatemala highland cities. El Mirador, the partially restored temple-pyramid that dominates the acropolis, overlooks the jewel-like Cenote Agua Azul 150 feet below. Some 200 unexcavated buildings make up Chinkultic, for little excavation and restoration have been done here. Yet its beautiful setting in the mountains and its easy access make Chinkultic worthy of a visit.

PALENQUE

Palenque, the most delicately magnificent of all restored Maya sites, nestles in the jungle on a natural terrace of the Sierra de Chiapas in southeastern Mexico. The ruins sit 200 feet above a swampy plain that stretches over 50 miles north to the Bay of Campeche.

Only a small portion of the ruins has been excavated. Many unexcavated buildings extend from the foot of the hills to several hundred feet above the Temple of the Inscriptions, and additional groups of unexcavated structures range for several miles along the north slope of the mountains in both directions from the center of the city.

As an important Classic Maya city, Palenque flowered from A.D. 600 to 800, perhaps because of its position on the northwestern frontier of the lowland Maya country that stretched from Copán in western Honduras through northern Guatemala and Belize to Uxmal and Chichén Itzá in Yucatán. The ruins are open to visitors and easily reached from Villahermosa.

The most striking Palenque structures are the Temple of Inscriptions, the Palace, and Lord Chan-Bahlum's three temples: Temple of the Cross, Temple of the Foliated Cross, and Temple of the Sun.

The Temple of the Inscriptions, a stepped pyramid with a broad, north-facing access stairway, houses the tomb of Pacal the Great (Lord Shield Pacal) (A.D. 615 to 683) and dominates the central zone. Down the stone stairway 80 feet below the temple floor, the Maya fashioned a sepulchre for the remains of Pacal. They covered this vault with a flat 12-foot long, 5-ton stone slab, carved with the figure of Pacal at the instant of death falling toward the Earth Monster. Three panels of glyphs inside the temple record the ancestral history,

beginning about A.D. 500, of the rulers of Palenque. The panels were designed as a demonstration of Pacal's divine origins. Palenque's many glyph panels have enabled Merle Greene Robertson, Linda Schele, David Stuart, and others to make great strides in deciphering Maya glyphic writing. Virtually all of Palenque's panels have been translated.

The Palace at Palenque sits on a rectangular platform about the size of an American city block. A four-storied tower, a structure unique among Maya buildings, rises from the center of the complex. Surrounding it, about eleven buildings had been constructed and remodeled over a span of more than 120 years by the kings of Palenque. The Palace served both as a residence for the king and his family and as an administrative center for the city-state.

The outer piers of this royal dwelling on the side facing the plaza bore modeled stucco relief figures depicting Pacal and other members of the royal family. In the northeast court are nine carved stone figures, all more than life-size, thought to represent both ancestral figures and captured rulers. The west side of that same court sports a hieroglyphic stairway that exhibits the date of Pacal's birth and his accession as king.

Pacal constructed the Temple of the Inscriptions. His son, Chan-Bahlum, constructed three other buildings: the temples of the Cross, the Foliated Cross, and the Sun. The glyphic texts and pictorial representations in all four temples present a declaration of the right to rule for each of these two kings by establishing the mythological base of their royal power.

Other buildings at Palenque were also constructed to aggrandize other kings and nobles of the city. The latest Maya Long-Count calendar date found at Palenque reads 9.18.9.4.4 (A.D. 799). By this time the flower of Palenque had almost withered. Trade languished and Palenque's influence had waned. By A.D. 820 Palenque was abandoned—overrun by Chontal Maya from the Tabasco plain.

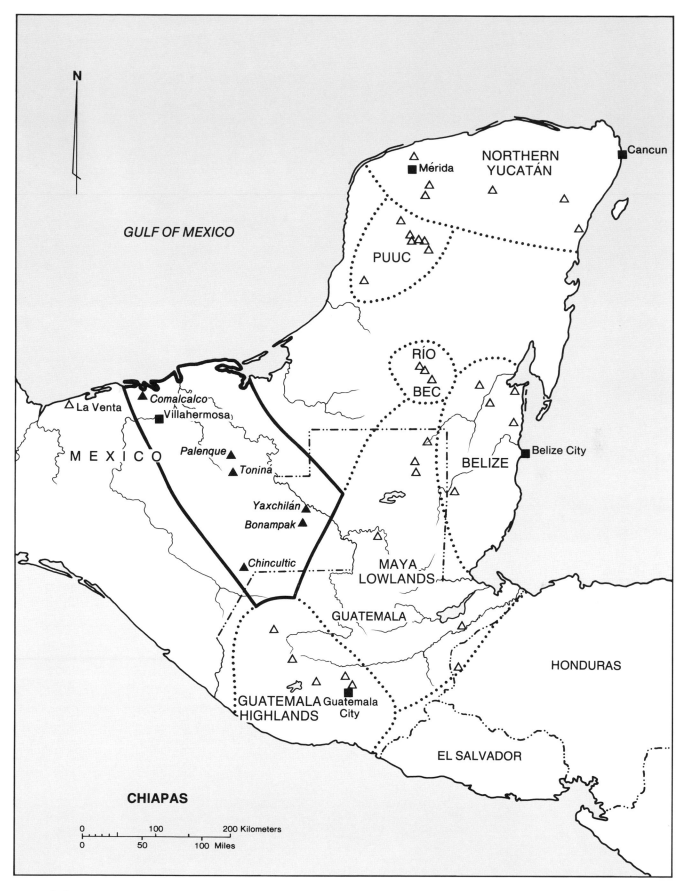

Map of Chiapas Maya Region.

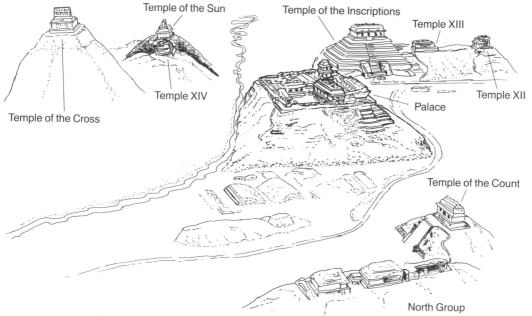

Temple of the Sun

Temple of the Cross

Temple XIV

Temple of the Inscriptions

Temple XIII

Temple XII

Palace

Temple of the Count

North Group

Palenque was built on the north slope of the Sierra de Chiapas in the late Classic. During the reigns of Lord Shield Pacal (A.D. 615–683) and his son Chan-Bahlum (A.D. 683–701), Palenque suddenly blossomed from a minor site into a principal Maya city of the western frontier.

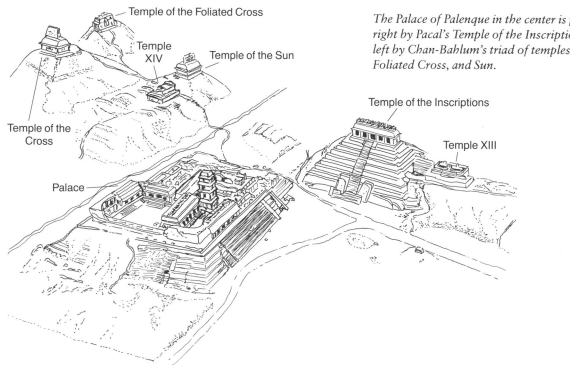

Temple of the Foliated Cross

Temple of the Cross

Temple XIV

Temple of the Sun

Temple of the Inscriptions

Temple XIII

Palace

The Palace of Palenque in the center is flanked on the right by Pacal's Temple of the Inscriptions and on the left by Chan-Bahlum's triad of temples: Cross, Foliated Cross, and Sun.

Above: Within the Temple of the Inscriptions (completed in A.D. 683) are three tablets of glyphs containing the ancestral history of the rulers of Palenque. Beneath the temple lies the grandiose crypt and sarcophagus of Pacal the Great (Lord Shield Pacal). Below: The crypt, containing Pacal the Great's remains lay 80 feet below the Temple of the Inscriptions. The stone stairway used to reach the crypt was filled with rubble after his death and the entrance on the temple floor was sealed. (From Morley and Brainerd, The Ancient Maya*).*

The vault encasing the remains of Pacal the Great, king of Palenque, was covered with a flat, 12-foot-long, 5-ton stone lid, decorated with the semireclining figure of Pacal and a schema of the cosmos as the Palencanos envisioned it. Pacal is represented at the instant of death, falling toward the Earth Monster. The slab iconography is an allegory of the earthly death and heavenly rebirth of the king. (Photograph by Merle Greene Robertson).

Above: The restored Palace at Palenque is about the size of an American city block and represents some 120 years of construction and remodeling. Its tower is unique in Maya architecture and it exhibits glyph-lined courts, decorated galleries, a hieroglyphic stairway, stucco relief figures, and life-sized, bas-relief sculptures. Below: Stucco relief figure of Pacal the Great and probably his mother, Lady Zac-Kuk, shown in the underworld (on pier d, Building D, of the palace). Building D was built during the reign of Kan Xul II, who became king in 702 and was captured by Toniná in 711.

Above: The Temple of the Sun, completed in A.D. 692, is part of Lord Chan-Bahlum's Temples of the Cross complex, built by the son of Pacal to manifest his power and authority as king. Below: These life-sized figures found in the northeast court of the Palace at Palenque represent subservient chiefs, or, more likely captives.

*Linda Schele's drawing interprets the bas-relief inside the
Temple of the Sun. Alongside the shield representing the Sun
God in the aspect of the Jaguar God of the Underworld stand
Pacal on the left and Chan-Bahlum on the right. The glyphs
above the shield record the date of Chan-Bahlum's inheritance
of power and his descent from Lord Shield Pacal and Lady
Ahpo-Hel.*

For many years it has been known that the glyphs on the Palenque Palace Hieroglyphic Stairway recorded the birth of Pacal the Great in A.D. 603 and his accession as king in 615. Linda Schele has recently deciphered the rest of the text together with the inscriptions on the wall flanking the stairway that describe the sacrifice of six captives referred to as "ritual brothers" from noble families of a defeated Maya city. This human sacrifice formed part of the dedication of Pacal's House C in the Palace. The stairway glyphs indicate the ceremony was witnessed by a brother of Shield Jaguar, king of Yaxchilán, a Maya city friendly to Palenque. The destructive effect of erosion on the exposed glyphic stairway can be seen here. The photograph in color was taken about twenty years before the black and white.

The east face of terraced pyramid, Temple I, at Comalcalco.

COMALCALCO

Comalcalco and Palenque (100 miles to the southeast) both bloomed late compared to other Maya Classic sites. They share similar temple styles and stucco facades, and we may assume both cities flourished for the two centuries immediately before abandonment around A.D. 800. Comalcalco sits on the northern edge of the water-logged Tabasco plain that extends from Palenque on the edge of the Chiapas Mountains to the Bahia de Campeche. The site lies in a series of rolling green hills, almost in sight of the sea, between the modern city of Villahermosa to the east and the oil town of Minatitlán to the west. Just to the west on the Tonalá River are the ruins of the very ancient Olmec city of La Venta, dead 1,000 years before Comalcalco arose.

The name "Comalcalco" comes from Nahuatl words meaning "in the house of the bricks." Within the two and one-half square mile archaeological zone, nearly 300 buildings, platforms, altars, elite residences, and residential mounds have been identified. During the A.D. 600s and 700s, Comalcalco's primary connections were with Palenque and the lowland Maya. Later, during the 900s, Comalcalco looked to the north and west with contacts with the Toltecs, Nahuas, and Totonacs of Mexico.

The ruins are dominated by an acropolis on a hill to the south, topped by the huge corbel-vaulted core that once supported the Palace. The Precolumbian people of the New World never discovered the principle of the true arch with a keystone; instead they spanned interior spaces by using a series of partially buried stone slabs, each successively higher row extending inward a bit more to create a triangular arch covered at the top with a capstone. Because of the lack of limestone nearby, Comalcalco builders employed thin kiln-fired slabs somewhat similar to the bricks of ancient Rome.

Below the Palace are Temples VI and VII. The south side of Temple VI displays a magnificent stucco mask. In the valley to the north of the Acropolis stands the partially restored stepped-pyramid, labeled Temple I, whose broad stairway faces east toward the great plaza.

Comalcalco represents one of the last hurrahs for the lowland Maya, both in its northwest frontier location of Mayaland and in its abandonment at the end of the Classic stage.

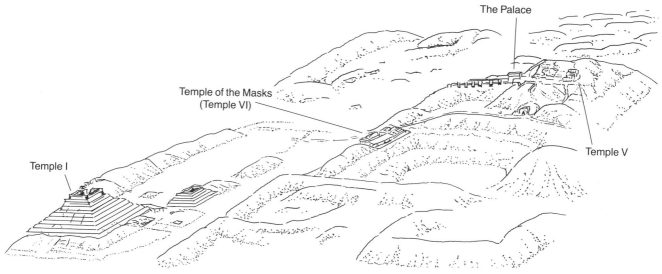

The Palace

Temple of the Masks
(Temple VI)

Temple I

Temple V

Comalcalco, some 50 miles west of Villahermosa, rests on rolling green hills near the Gulf Coast. This late Classic Maya site was closely connected to Palenque. The great pyramid, Temple I, faces a long plaza extending to the east. To the south (right) is the Acropolis topped by the ruins of the Palace. Comalcalco's buildings were constructed of kiln-fired brick rather than the limestone found at other Maya cities.

This view of Comalcalco from south to north shows the Gulf of Mexico in the distance. In the foreground is the Palace. Temple VI, containing a well-preserved stucco mask, lies in the center between the Palace and Temple I.

Above: From the Palace, there is a spectacular view across Temples VI and VII to Temple I in the valley below the Acropolis. Below: Stucco mask.

Above: Toniná is a beautifully situated, small, late Maya Classic site near Ocosingo, Mexico, between Palenque and San Cristóbal de las Casas. Some restoration has been done since *this 1983 photograph. Below: Crowning the steep hillside at the 7th level, the Temple of the Prisoners dominates the ruin filled slope of the Maya city of Toniná.*

The excavated Palace sits atop a recently excavated stone-mosaic facade.

The Great Plaza at the foot of the structure filled hillside contains Toniná's major ballcourt on the east side, the large Warriors Mound in the center, several platforms, and a small *ballcourt in the northwest corner of the plaza with several nearby stelae and altars.*

YAXCHILÁN

Another major Maya city, Yaxchilán, was built on the terraced banks of the Usumacinta. Its only modern-day access other than by boat consists of a short, narrow airstrip with high underbrush along both sides. The banks of the river rise steeply at this point preventing any approach to the airstrip from the Guatemala side. The trick in making a landing at Yaxchilán is to select a landmark on the cliffs on the Guatemala side of the river while the plane is still about 1,000 feet above the jungle, then let down inside the cliffs to the north of the ruins and follow the river just above the water until reaching the landmark; at that moment bank the plane into a sharp right turn, drop the flaps, land, then set the brakes hard since the strip is so short.

A visit to Yaxchilán is worth the trouble. On terraces covered with luxuriant tropical forest endure the ruins of a wonderful city. Yaxchilán has no temple-pyramids of the Tikal variety, but rather displays mansard-style buildings with roof combs similar to those at Palenque. The location of the buildings on terraces, one above the other, gives the effect of temples standing atop pyramids. Scattered throughout the ruins are magnificently carved stelae, altars, and panels in bas-relief.

Yaxchilán is well known to scholars, however, because of the great breakthrough Tatiana Proskouriakoff made there and at Piedras Negras across the river in analyzing dated monuments. Her work in the 1950s and 1960s opened a whole new world of Maya glyph translation and demonstrated that the figures long thought to be gods and priests were in fact kings, queens, and nobles.

At Yaxchilán, inscriptions on the many stone lintels revealed a range of Maya bloodletting ceremonies: during astronomical events, for ancestor worship, and period endings. Carolyn Tate, who recently completed her doctoral dissertation on Yaxchilán, reports that all of the kings of Yaxchilán are now known—seventeen of them with the possibility of another king who ruled during the middle Classic when there was a gap in the erection of monuments. All the kings belonged to either the Jaguar or the Skull family. These two lineages alternated over the centuries. The first ruler for whom we have a date, a Jaguar, began his reign about A.D. 337, and the last known ruler, a Skull, was on the throne in A.D. 800. Women were well reported at Yaxchilán—nine are mentioned in the glyphs.

Shield Jaguar and his son Bird Jaguar IV reigned during the middle 700s. Carved stone lintels recount the capture of Jeweled Skull from another city by Bird Jaguar. Following the custom of Maya princes, Bird Jaguar erected a monument to glorify himself as a powerful king able to capture, humiliate, torture, and sacrifice another city's ruler.

Bird Jaguar IV was Yaxchilán's most prolific builder. During his 20-year reign, he constructed thirteen buildings, thirty lintels, Stelae 1 and 9, and the Stalagmite stela in front of Building 33. His Building 33 was constructed to face the summer solstice and by doing so, Tate believes, he was making a cosmological statement to his people about his control of the movements of the sun. His grandson was the last king of Yaxchilán.

The short, narrow, sod airstrip is the most feasible access to Yaxchilán. The strip lies in a deep canyon on the west side of the Usumacinta River.

The late Maya Classic House of Hachakyum (Structure 33) overlooks the Great Plaza that parallels the river. Yaxchilán in late Classic times (600s and 700s) was ruled by the Jaguar family. Bird Jaguar IV, who became king in 752, is responsible for much of the extant building.

Structure 33 faces east toward the Usumacinta River. Dedicated in A.D. 756, it depicts scenes from the life of Bird Jaguar.

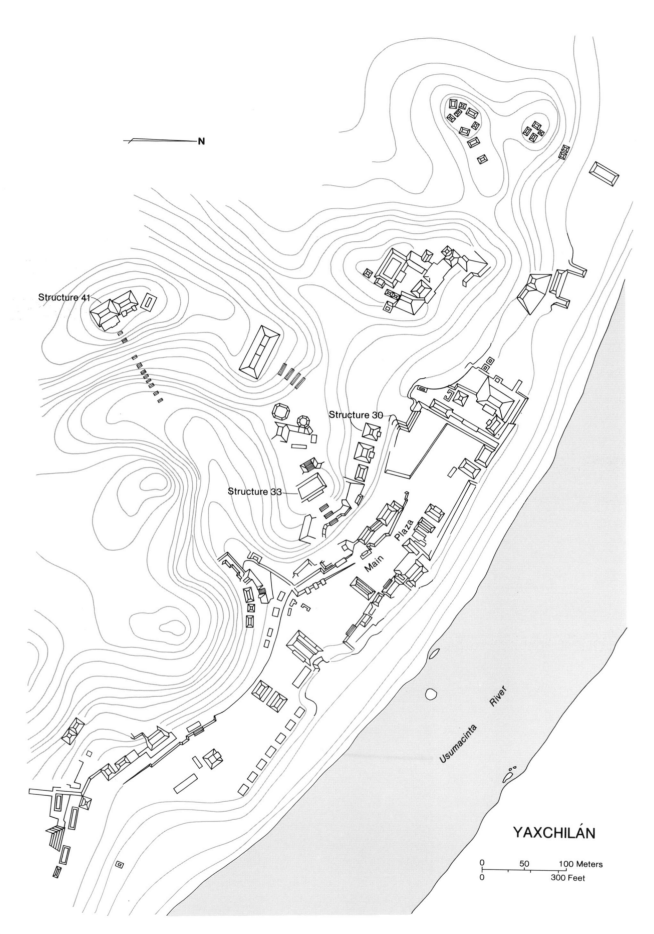

Structure 41

Structure 30

Structure 33

Main
Plaza

Usumacinta   River

YAXCHILÁN

0		50		100 Meters
0			300 Feet	

Yaxchilán plan.

Right: House of Hachakyum and Stela 31 at the lower right. Below: Structure 19 faces the Great Plaza and contains nine vaulted chambers connected by sixteen vaulted passageways on three levels. Four doors and three niches are visible here.

Yaxchilán Buildings: A view of the back of Structure 30.

Structures 41, 40 and 39. (Photograph by Carolyn Tate.)

Structure 40. (Photograph by Carolyn Tate.)

Bird Jaguar IV's Stela 1, Yaxchilán.

Left: Bird Jaguar IV (on the right) faces Shield Jaguar. Stela 11, dated June 22, 741, originally stood in front of Structure 40 at Yaxchilán, but the Mexican government attempted to move it to Mexico City for the 1964 opening of the Museo Nacional de Antropologia. It proved too heavy to move with the available equipment and now lies to the east of Structure 5. Below: The glyph panel at the base of Stela 11 records the accession of Bird Jaguar IV, names Shield Jaguar and Lady Ik Skull as his parents, and therefore demonstrates his right to rule.

Above: Yaxchilán. The hieroglyphic stairway in front of Structure 33, steps 7 and 8, depicts the ballgame. The stairway was erected by Bird Jaguar IV. Right: A Maya nobleman, whose name does not survive, is depicted as a secondary figure on Stela 7 done by Shield Jaguar II around 9.17.5.0.0 (A.D. 775).

Above: Bonampak, city of King Chaan-muan. Structure 3 is to the left and Structure 1 (the covered building containing the famous murals) is on the right, fronted by Stela 1. Below: Stela 1 stands in the foreground of this small classic Maya site that is the locale of the magnificent murals first photographed by Giles G. Healy in 1946.

Above right: Chaan-muan's Stela 1 dates from around A.D. 780 and stands some 16 feet high. Left: Detail of the figure depicting ruler Chaan-muan of Bonampak carved on Stela 1. Below: This portion of the spectacular murals at Bonampak shows the torture and sacrifice of captives. Resplendently dressed ruler Chaan-muan, flanked by his court, stands in the center at the top of the stairway. To his right (at the edge of the mural) are captives, whose fingernails are being torn out probably as a prelude to execution. Mary Ellen Miller places this event a few days after August 2, 792, on the day of the heliacal rising of Venus, a propitious time for sacrifice.

Chinkultic, occupied in Preclassic times and later by the Maya in the late Classic and early Postclassic, lies just off the Pan-American Highway near the Guatemala-Mexican border. Its setting in the high country surrounded by forests and lakes is one of the most spectacular of any Mesoamerican site.

CHINKULTIC

This beautiful ruin sits in the mountains south and east of San Cristóbal de las Casas near the Mexican-Guatemalan border. Chinkultic's first occupation began in the late Preclassic during the 125 years between 50 B.C. and A.D. 75 and extended to A.D. 300–350 in early Classic times. It was a highland city, Maya, but with a different culture from the Maya of the Preclassic lowlands. Situated nearly astride the continental divide, Chincultic was a gateway for trade with the lowland Maya of Chiapas, the Guatemala Highlanders all the

way to El Salvador, and the Izapans on the Pacific coast in the region around what is now Tapachula, Mexico.

The city was abandoned from the middle 300s to around 700 when it was reoccupied by late Classic Maya who erected stelae and a ballcourt in the traditional Maya fashion. Construction waned in the 900s, but the city continued to be occupied well into the Postclassic to around A.D. 1250.

In addition to its magnificent alpine location, the deep, sparkling, Cenote Azul adds to the beauty and uniqueness of Chinkultic. The cenote served during the centuries both as a receptical for ritual offerings and for

El Mirador at Chinkultic.

refuse disposal. Ceramic vessels, an underwater platform, a stone mask, green stone beads, obsidian blades, a vase with a Chac image, and incense burners found in the cenote suggest ritual offerings, especially by the Preclassic and early Classic people. There has been no evidence of human sacrifice, however, such as has been found at the Chichén Itzá cenote. A jawbone complete with teeth is the only trace of human remains yet discovered.

The restored Group A is dominated by El Mirador (Temple I). There are about 200 mounds divided into six groups that make up the Chinkultic ruins.

CHAPTER SIX

Guatemala Highlands

The major ruins along the spine of the active volcanic mountains composing the Sierra Madre in Guatemala fit the late Postclassic Mexican-Maya stage: Utatlán, Iximché, Zaculeu, and Mixco Viejo. The beautifully green volcanoes, many still adorned by wisps of smoke curling from their peaks, seem so symmetrical they could have been drawn by children. These ruins, close to the Pan-American Highway between the Mexican border and Guatemala City, once were warring cities, built in defensive positions on the tops of mountain ridges. They were still inhabited when the Spanish *conquistadores* led by the ruthless Pedro de Alvarado conquered and destroyed them.

The sparse ruins of the Quiché Maya capital at Utatlán—burned by Alvarado in 1524—lie near the modern Quiché center at Chichicastenango. Tourists come here from all over the world on market day to see the unreconstructed and independent Maya trade their produce and burn copal on the steps of the Catholic church like their forebears did on the steps of temple-pyramids.

Iximché was the Cakchiquel Maya capital. In Postclassic times the local population submitted to the rule of dynasties from Mexico who arrived during the 1000s. M. D. Coe suggests some of the Toltecs exiled from Tula, along with Topiltzin Quetzalcoatl, could have come here while others conquered Yucatán and rebuilt Chichén Itzá. The Annals of the Cakchiquels speak of Tula as their homeland and the architecture has a distinct Mexican flavor: Aztec-type, twin pyramid-temples; Mexican ballcourts, with their vertical sides; and post-

and-lintel rather than corbel arch roofs. Iximché's excavation and restoration was carried out during the 1960s by the Guatemalan Society for Anthropology and History under the direction of Jorge Guillemin.

Mam-Maya-speaking people constructed Zaculeu, with a heavy Mexican influence, beginning in early Classic times, although most of the building took place between A.D. 900–1200. Later they fortified the city, but it fell to Gonzalo de Alvarado in 1525 after a bloody siege. During the 1940s, the United Fruit Company sponsored restoration of Zaculeu by Aubrey Trik, Richard Woodbury, and John Dimick.

The Pokoman Maya builders of Mixco Viejo selected an almost impregnable series of ridges for their capital city in the forest-covered mountains about 30 miles north of Guatemala City. The Musee de l'Homme of Paris excavated and restored the site during the 1950s and 1960s, but, unfortunately, some of the reconstruction was damaged by an earthquake in the 1970s.

The very early cultures of the highlands of Guatemala—Abaj Takalik and El Baul—formed a conduit through which many of the customs and traditions of the Olmec (800–300 B.C.) and Izapans (300 B.C.–A.D. 150) came to Kaminaljuyú. As a Preclassic city (the ruins have been engulfed by modern Guatemala City), Kaminaljuyú dominated the highlands between 300 B.C. and A.D. 150. The city's roots extended back at least a millennium before the Christian Era. Its inhabitants spoke the Maya tongue and numbered between 25,000 and 50,000 during its halcyon days. Some attributes funneled through Kaminaljuyú to the Classic Maya: include the aggrandizement of rulers on stone stelae, elaborate headdresses, bloodletting self-sacrifice, the bar-and-dot numeration system and calendar, glyphic writing, and perhaps the roots of the Maya language. This early Maya city languished and fell into ruin by A.D. 300.

Some time around A.D. 400, Kaminaljuyú and the Guatemala highlands came under the influence and domination of Teotihuacán from the Valley of Mexico, some 800 miles to the northwest. The old Maya city of Kaminaljuyú was then rebuilt in the image of Teotihuacán using the *talud-tablero*-style temples topped with post-and-lintel roofs, butterfly goddesses, and figures with speech scrolls. As time progressed the elite became Mayanized. Curl Nose, who became king of Tikal in A.D. 379, may have come from Kaminaljuyú. This domination lasted until around A.D. 600 when the history of the highlands becomes misty until the rise of the late Classic city-states. However, we suspect Mexican peoples governed the highlands during the times between the fall of Teotihuacán and the arrival of the Spaniards.

An excellent model of Mixco Viejo sits at the entrance to the ruins. The Spaniards were able to conquer thousands of Indians with only a few hundred men because of long-standing conflicts between the city states of the Guatemalan highlands and the ravages of Old World diseases introduced to the New World in 1521.

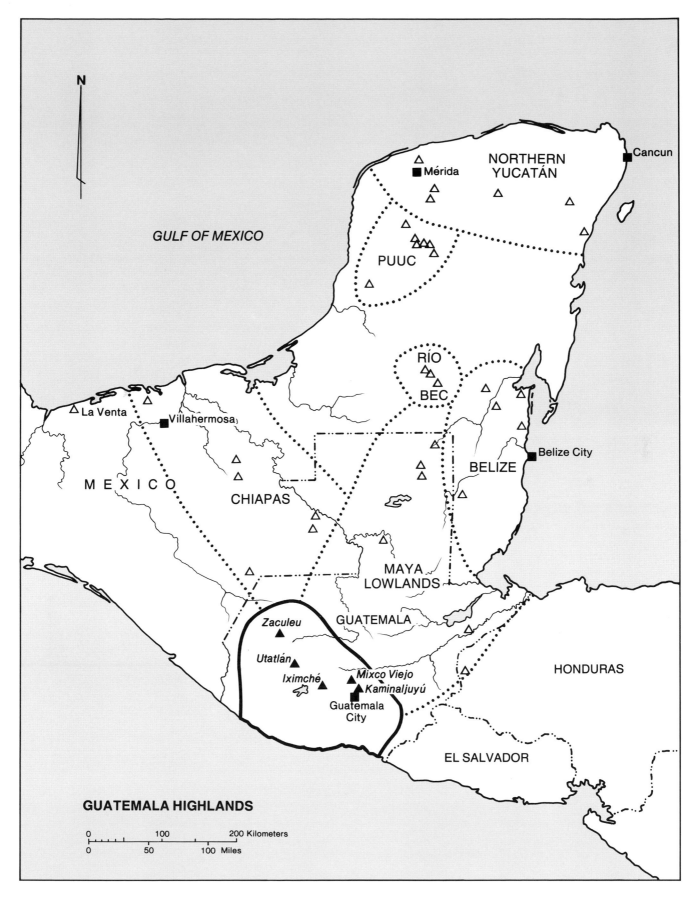

Major sites of the highland region of Guatemala. These sites, occupied at the time of the Spanish conquest in the 1500s, existed just at the beginning of Mesoamerican historical times.

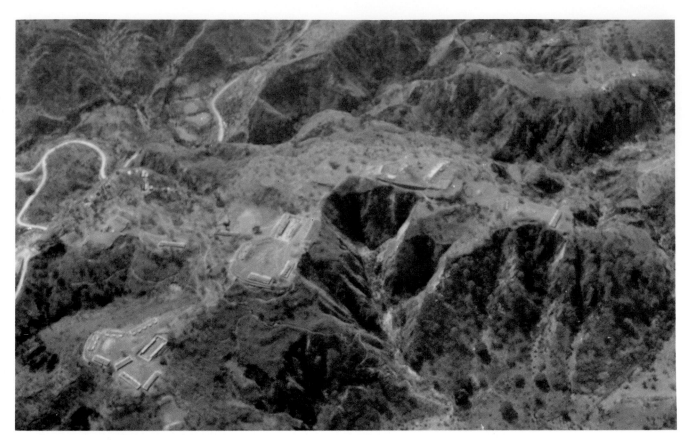

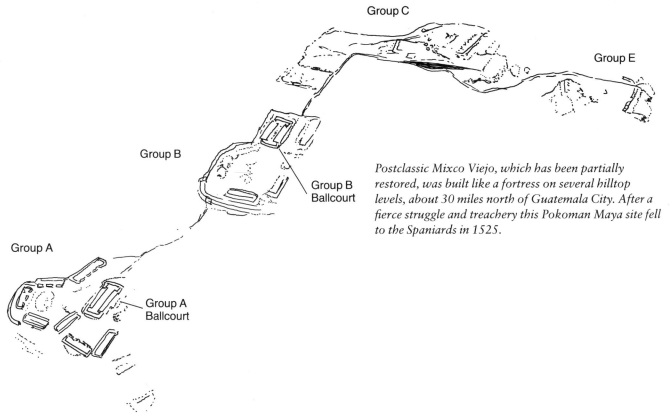

Group C

Group E

Group B

Group B
Ballcourt

*Postclassic Mixco Viejo, which has been partially
restored, was built like a fortress on several hilltop
levels, about 30 miles north of Guatemala City. After a
fierce struggle and treachery this Pokoman Maya site fell
to the Spaniards in 1525.*

Group A

Group A
Ballcourt

Above: The ballcourt (Group A) during restoration in 1979. Right: Some of the restoration work done in the 1950s and 1960s at Mixco Viejo was severely damaged by earthquakes in the late 1970s.

Iximché's beautiful ruins are situated near the Pan-American Highway, about 50 miles west of Guatemala City. The Cakchiquel Maya of Iximché furnished warriors to help the Spaniards defeat the Quiché Maya. Soon afterward the Spaniards conquered their city too.

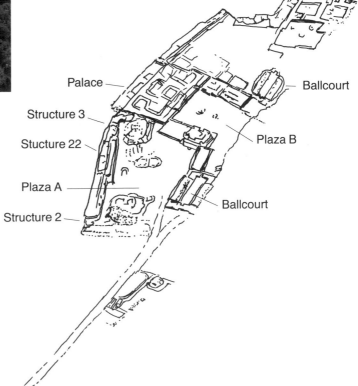

Palace

Structure 3

Stucture 22

Plaza A

Structure 2

Ballcourt

Plaza B

Ballcourt

Above: At the center of Iximché the Cakchiquels built an imposing palace. Structure 3 in Plaza A joined the palace on the northwest. Right: Plaza B and Altar 14 were located in front of the palace to the southwest. Below: Plaza A, Structure 2.

The Quiché Maya of Utatlán were conquered by the Spaniards with the help of the Cakchiquels and other highland Indians; their chieftains were burned alive, and Utatlán—capital of the Quiché Maya empire—was completely destroyed.

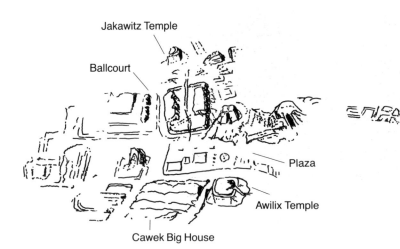

Jakawitz Temple

Ballcourt

Plaza

Awilix Temple

Cawek Big House

Unrestored Utatlán is still used as a ceremonial center by the Quiché Maya. It was once a beautiful city of temples and palaces. Here we are looking through the ancient ballcourt toward the Awilix temple at the upper left, the Cawek Big House in the center, and the Jakawitz temple ruins under the trees at the right.

Zaculeu, the Mam-Maya religious center with heavy Mexican architectural influence, was occupied primarily after A.D. 900. In the 1400s it was conquered by the Quiché Maya who named the site Zaculeu (White Earth), but by the time of the Spanish conquest it had been recovered by the Mam. The site, near the Guatemalan town of Huehuetenango, was restored under the sponsorship of the United Fruit Company in the 1940s.

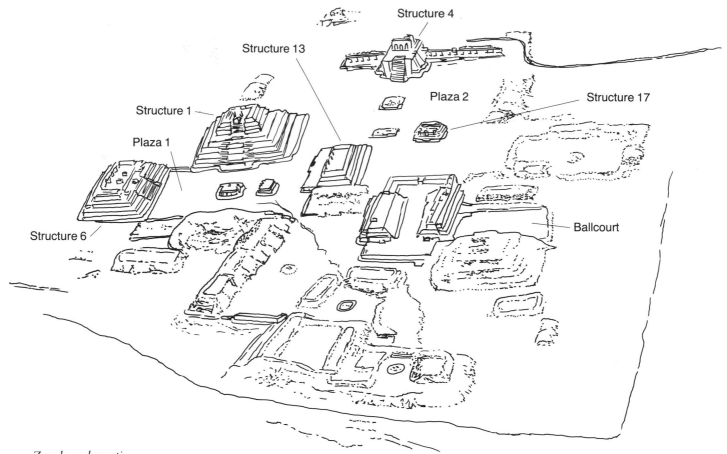

Structure 4

Structure 13

Structure 1

Plaza 1

Structure 6

Plaza 2

Structure 17

Ballcourt

Zaculeu schematic.

Above: Tiered pyramid, Structure 1, at Zaculeu. Below: Zaculeu's ballcourt lies between Plazas 4 and 8 with the playing alley (about 80 feet long and 22 feet wide) running roughly east and west. On the sides of the alley were low vertical walls, a battered bench, and sloping walls topped by Buildings 22 and 23.

Above: Plaza I viewed from the southwest looking toward Structure 6. Below: Plaza I and Building 13 seen from Structure 6.

Above: Structure 4 situated in the southeast corner of the ruins of Zaculeu. Below: Structure 17. After a long siege, Caibil Balam surrendered to Alvarado in October 1525. Although the city was never occupied thereafter, it continued to be a place of worship for the Mam.

CHAPTER SEVEN

Río Bec Region

North of the Petén of Guatemala in southern Campeche and Quintana Roo, Mexico, lies the Río Bec region of the ancient Maya. The buildings at these ruins, mostly from late Classic Maya times (A.D. 550–850), display a distinctive architectural style. The Río Bec style differs markedly from other Maya construction, consisting of rubble-filled, stone-faced pyramids (with stairways too steep to climb), topped with Petén-like temples that are filled solid. These false temples are faced with simulated doors leading nowhere. In effect they were nothing more than ornamental towers—their entire being constituted a stage setting, built to emulate full-fledged temples at other cities. The south pyramid at Río Bec contains an inner stairway and a tomb, making the pyramid functional as a mausoleum. Although at least thirty-eight Río Bec sites are known, we show three that are accessible to visitors: Río Bec B, Becan, and Xpuhil. These three sites exemplify the Río Bec architectural style; each has single-story, range-type rooms embellished by two or three towers constructed to simulate temple-pyramids.

There were no large cities in the Río Bec region. The Río Bec sites occupy a region of nearly trackless, thick virgin forest. On the flight from Palenque northeast to Chetumal, the first 60 miles reveal a few roads and villages; but the next 180 miles to Chetumal disclose nothing but a sea of green vegetation with no landmarks, no villages, no trails, and no roads except for the single ribbon of Highway 186 running east from the village of Escárcega to Chetumal. Not far from the narrow cut made by the highway in the undergrowth stand the ruins of Becan, Xpuhil, Chicanná, and Río Bec B.

RÍO BEC B

Temple B at Río Bec is a beautiful twin-towered building hidden in the forest of trees and tangled vines about 20 miles south of Xpuhil on Highway 186 (between Escárcega and Chetumal). Temple B (late Classic Maya, A.D. 700–850) belongs to a scattered group of ruins including some ten groups within a 30-square-mile area. All these groups together bear the label Río Bec, but they do not necessarily constitute a single village or site. French archaeologist Maurice de Perigny, who discovered the structure Río Bec A in 1906, called the site Río Beque for the small ephemeral stream nearby. Raymond E. Merwin and Clarence L. Hay discovered Río Bec B in 1912.

After the 1912 expedition, Río Bec B literally disappeared. During the 1930s several attempts were made by the Carnegie Institution of Washington to relocate it. New ruins associated with the site were discovered, but Río Bec B could not be found. It was finally rediscovered in May 1973 by a documentary film team from Princeton led by Hugh and Suzanne Johnston and accompanied by Gillett Griffin and Andrea Seuffert.

The site was quite difficult for us to find from the air. We located it by flying to the spot indicated on the map and then initiating a square search of the kind used by John Q. Royce when he was an aircraft carrier squadron commander in the Pacific during World War II. It took us about 20 minutes flying time to find the beautiful little temple nestled in a small clearing in the forest.

Río Bec B has survived for 1,200 years with relatively little destruction by the jungle. The architectural eye-catchers of this temple—or perhaps temple-palace—are the two 55-foot-high towers constructed to look like pyramids topped with temples similar to those at Tikal in the Petén. In reality, however, they were built for show. The front steps are impossible to climb because they incline only about 8° from the vertical, and the false doorways at the top, both front and rear, lead into solid masses of masonry and rubble. The monster mask facades do not decorate temples; instead, they adorn solid rubble towers with rounded edges garnished with stone facings to make them look like temple-pyramids. These towers provide beautifully proportioned embellishments to the rooms below.

The lower structure consists of six rooms built upon a low platform—two in the center (one behind the other with a central doorway on the east side accessed by a short stairway) and four smaller rooms in the rear. Roof combs rise from the medial wall in the center of the building rather than at the top of the temple-pyramids, marking another unusual aspect of Río Bec B.

BECAN

Becan, located on Highway 186 about 73 miles west of Chetumal at the foot of the Yucatán Peninsula, is easily accessible.

Pottery indicates the Becan site has been occupied since the middle Preclassic, but the construction spurt did not begin until the end of the late Preclassic (A.D. 250) when the defensive dry moat—for which Becan is famous—was constructed. This ditch ran about 16 feet deep and 32 feet wide, and when added to the embankment it created a nearly 40-foot-high defensive barrier surrounding about 47 acres of the city. Seven causeways (sacbeob) radiated from the center of the site. The ruins of Becan sit on a limestone outcropping rising about 30 feet higher than the surrounding flatland of underbrush and trees dotted by cleared milpas for farming.

Becan was a fortified Classic Maya settlement. Archaeologists speculate that this site served as a defense against the Petén Maya to the south or, alternatively, it may have been a fortified outpost of the Petén Maya. R.E.W. Adams speculates the Becan fortress could have been a Teotihuacán outpost since indications of Mexican highland influence in early Classic times have been found, particularly at Tikal and recently at Río Azul.

Most of the buildings visible today were constructed during the late Classic (A.D. 550–850). The major part of the reconstruction and restoration is in the elevated Southeast Plaza. Structure I bounds the Southeast Plaza on the south. On the east and west sides of this building the Maya constructed two massive towers

in the Río Bec style. However, there is no indication that these towers were surmounted by simulated temples nor were they decorated with sculptures. Across the Southeast Plaza from the twin-towered Structure I stands Structure IV. A grand staircase mounts the side of this building. On the top of Structure IV are several rooms surrounding a small courtyard. Some relief sculpture also adorns the south face of the standing walls. To the north of Structure IV lies the Central Plaza, surrounded by unexcavated structures. A twin-towered building on the east side (Structure VIII) was also reached by a monumental stairway from plaza level. On the north side of the Central Plaza is Structure IX, a pyramid about 100 feet high that probably was faced with a stairway and topped by a temple.

Becan was never large enough to be a regional Maya center, but it had at least a 1,200-year existence extending into the Postclassic. Building ceased about A.D. 830, but Becan continued to be occupied until 1200.

XPUHIL

Xpuhil, about 70 miles west of Chetumal, represents typical late Classic Río Bec style. The ruined temple (Structure I of Group I) has three towers originally faced with incredibly steep stairways and false temples complete with roof combs and doorways leading nowhere. These buildings appear to be reproductions of the pyramid-temples of Tikal and other cities in the Petén to the south, but they were simulated reproductions only—built to look like their Petén models. Monster masks top the "temple" doors and serpent jaws adorn the sides. Between the two forward pyramids stood a highly decorated three-door, six-room building, the facade of which consisted of three monster masks.

Additional ruins lie scattered nearby. When Karl Ruppert and John Denison first discovered the ruin in the 1930s, it was in a better state of preservation than now, which allowed Tatiana Proskouriakoff to produce an accurate restoration drawing. The back side of the west pyramid is now the best preserved portion of the ruin.

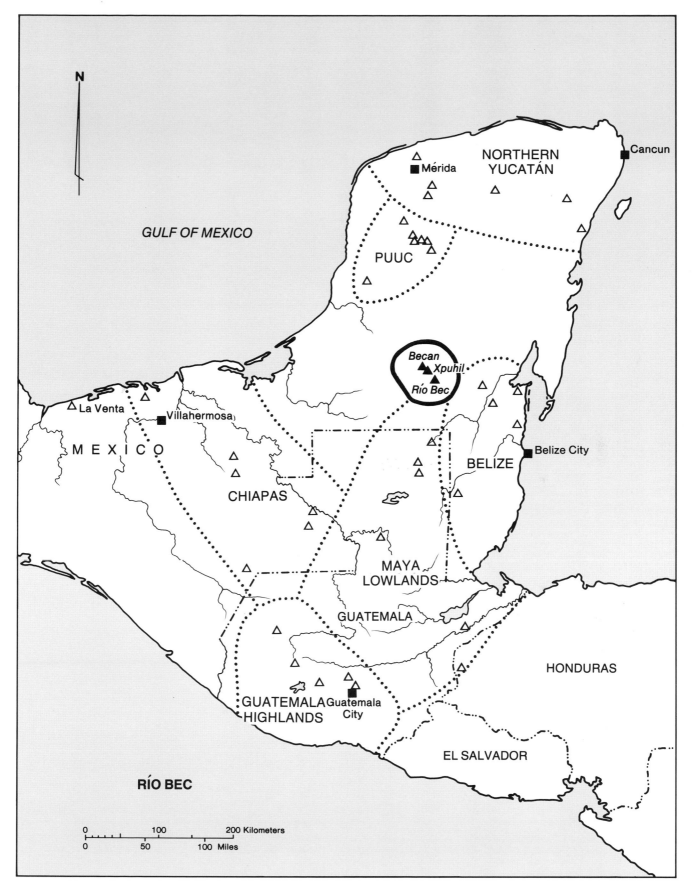

Map of the Río Bec region.

Above: The Río Bec B ruin, so well hidden in the jungle of the southern Yucatán Peninsula of Mexico that it was lost to archaeologists from 1912 to 1973, displays an exquisite, small, late Classic Maya palace flanked by towers. This view from the west shows two towers and two roof combs. Below: Río Bec B towers were constructed to resemble pyramids crowned with temples in the style of the Petén, but they were built for show with false stairways and false temples as embellishments to the palace below.

Mexican Highway 186 between Chetumal and Escárcega passes close by Becan and Xpuhil. Becan was a fortified Maya town; principal construction began around A.D. 250. Structure I in the center, with its two massive ruined towers, bounds the southeast plaza on the south. Across the plaza in the background is Structure IV. These buildings are Maya late Classic dating from A.D. 550–850.

Above: Structure IV at Becan occupies the north side of the plaza and faces Structure I with its massive Río Bec–style towers. Structure IV's grand stairway, one of the widest in Mayaland, gave access to an elite residential complex on the top of the pyramid. From the top one can gain the same view across the top of the forest canopy that greeted the ancient Maya. Below: Structure III closes off the east end of Becan's Southeast Plaza, in front of which is a small circular platform or altar.

Xpuhil, a late Classic Maya site located 3 miles east of Becan, evidences the Río Bec architectural device of purely decorative towers built to look like real temple-pyramids. Above: East view. Below: West view.

Above: Tatiana Proskouriakoff's reconstruction of Xpuhil shows three vaulted, one-story rooms surrounded by three pyramid-towers. Each pyramid was topped with monster masks. Although similar in style to Petén pyramids that have a temple and roof comb at the summit, these three pyramids were built in late Classic Maya Río Bec style without functional stairways or temples. Below: Xpuhil, the Maya word for "place of the cattails," was probably so-named because of a nearby aguada, or water hole. Group I, shown from the east, was composed of three towers and a one-story, palace-type building. Only the columns remain. Each of the towers originally displayed Chenes-style masks.

This view of the west side of Structure I shows a portion of the false stairway, a Chenes-style mask, and the false temple. The facades of Xpuhil's temples were finished with carefully fitted, carved stone masonry.

A close-up view of the mask on the false stairway of Structure I at Xpuhil shows the intricate details created by the Maya stonemasons.

Left: Chicanná, discovered in 1966, is a small late Classic Maya site buried in the jungle south of Highway 186, a few miles southwest of Becan. This palace on the north side of a plaza is one of two structures that have been cleared of vegetation and rubble. Below: Structure II at Chicanná, built between A.D. 750 and 770, was excavated and consolidated by Jack Eaton in 1970. The portal of this temple is an open monster's mouth flanked by profile monster masks.

CHAPTER EIGHT

Puuc Region

The Puuc constitutes a string of low hills, not more than 350 feet high, beginning about 45 miles south of Mérida and ranging east-west in the northern part of the otherwise flat Yucatán Peninsula. Among these hills lie a series of late Classic Maya sites including Uxmal, Kabah, Xlapak, Sayil, Labná, Chacmultún, and, to the south, Etzná. Both the region and the architectural style have long been referred to as Puuc.

Puuc cities flourished for 150 years between A.D. 770 and 925—the same period that marked the decline and abandonment of the Classic Maya cities to the south. This shift, the rise of the Maya north and the decline of the Maya south, was due in no small part to the Chontal or Putun Itzá Maya traders from the southern coast of the Gulf of Mexico who traded goods between the cities of highland Mexico and Yucatán. They, with the aid of their Mexican trading partners, cut the old trade routes of the southern Maya and created new trading centers in Yucatán at places such as Dzibilchaltún and Chichén Itzá. In the Puuc, the Maya prospered as traders and farmers who produced cotton and other agricultural products to trade for salt, slaves, honey, obsidian, and high-status goods.

Jeff Kowalski points out that the close connection between the Chontal traders and the Mexican cities (such as Cacaxtla, Xochicalco, and Tula) may have been responsible for the Mexican-looking aspects of Puuc architecture: the feathered serpent and the skull-and-bones motifs.

Recent research indicates that the Chontal Itzá assumed control of Chichén Itzá around A.D. 866 under the leadership of Kakupacal. From that time on, Chichén Itzá became an intense rival of the Puuc cities; the rivalry culminated in the defeat and abandonment of the Puuc centers during the late 900s around the time of the Toltec takeover of Chichén Itzá. The Classic Maya era ended with the demise of the Puuc cities.

The earliest Puuc architecture is found at Etzná and dates from A.D. 600–750. Certain characteristics set Puuc buildings apart from other Maya architectural creations: round columns, with entasis (slight swelling in the center) for visual effect, and square capitals, placed in doorways; long rows of half-columns as part of the facades; intricate mosaic facades with stepped frets; panels of hook-nose deities, probably representations of Chac (the Maya Rain God) but in some cases the Sky Serpent; the head of a human or deity emerging from a serpent's mouth; and the frequent use of veneers of thin limestone squares over rubble-cored buildings. Each of these sites had huge, bottle-shaped cisterns—called *chultunes*—beneath the plazas or as part of the buildings. These cisterns provided water during the six-month dry season.

The Puuc builders did not usually cluster temple-pyramids around plazas, nor did they regularly practice the stela cult, although some stelae occur. The theme of Puuc architecture is a plain, lower-front wall with an upper facade alive with geometric designs and stylized masks of deities. The public buildings were scattered throughout the site and were probably interspersed with habitations. Puuc architects also constructed gigantic, multistoried palace platforms in layers, like wedding cakes. Each successive layer was a honeycomb of rubble-filled spaces indented from the layer below. Along the front of each layer they constructed a series of vaulted rooms. Superficially, these platforms appear to be multistoried buildings, but in reality they are solid rubble-cored platforms with facades of stone masonry chambers. Most of the platforms were topped with palaces, but they similarly constructed a five-tiered pyramid at Etzná supporting a temple at the top. Despite their similarities in style, each of the many Puuc sites has individual characteristics.

UXMAL

Uxmal lies about 50 miles south of Mérida, the capital of the state of Yucatán, on the northern edge of the Puuc Hills. Those interested in the Maya will find this big, 1,000-year-old Puuc site enchanting. It is easily accessible and well maintained, has excellent accommodations for tourists nearby, and displays beautiful Puuc- and Chenes-style buildings with superb stonework. The surrounding vegetation is brown in winter (the dry season) and lush green during the rainy months of spring and summer. The dense forest is interrupted by *milpas*, fields of the modern Maya, who like their ancestors had done for thousands of years cut away and burn the underbrush for the planting of crops.

Relatively little is known about the kings of the Puuc cities, but recent research by Jeff Kowalski indicates that Lord Chac-Uinal-Kan and his son Lord Chac were rulers of Uxmal in the late A.D. 800s. Lord Chac is the central figure on the facade of the House of the Governor, constructed around 900.

It is impossible to say whether the rulers of the Puuc cities were native Puuc nobles or outsiders who imposed their authority on the local Maya. The architecture suggests they were Maya, although some of the stone reliefs (such as the feathered serpent and the skull-and-bones carvings) indicate some influence of the Putun Itzá Maya who, with their Mexican connections, had ruled Chichén Itzá since the middle 800s. References at Uxmal to Lady Kuk, mother of Kakupacal of Chichén Itzá, indicate a relationship between the two cities in the late 800s. Things may not always have been harmonious, however; the recent discovery of a wall that originally encircled portions of central Uxmal may indicate periods of warfare.

The construction dates for the buildings at Uxmal, and for the other Puuc cities as well, fall between the late 700s and the early 900s. The Puuc cities were late Classic Maya and flourished while their counterparts in the south were being abandoned. The Dovecote, one of the earlier buildings, dates from the A.D. 700s; the latest recorded date from the Nunnery is 905; and the later

buildings, such as the House of the Governor, considered the epitome of Puuc architecture, may have been constructed around 900. Although there is a legend that Uxmal was occupied by the Xiu family as one of the centers of the League of Mayapán (Uxmal, Chichén Itzá, and Mayapán) in Postclassic times, the archaeological evidence indicates that Uxmal was abandoned before the Toltecs occupied Chichén Itzá or Mayapán was constructed. Before it was abandoned in the late 900s, Uxmal may have been home to more than 20,000 people.

The excavated portion of Uxmal lies on a north-south axis with the Great Pyramid and House of the Governor to the south and the Nunnery Quadrangle and Pyramid of the Magician to the north. Uxmal had several pyramid-plaza complexes similar to Palenque and Tikal. A series of three plazas extends northward from the Southwest Pyramid through the Dovecote. Another plaza is made up of the Pyramid of the Magician and the Nunnery complex.

The distinctive qualities of the Puuc and Chenes styles may be seen in both construction and decoration. The buildings have a core of rubble, faced with expertly cut stones. The wall stones were pecked smooth and closely fitted and required little plaster covering. Generally, the sculptural decoration was limited to the upper facade. The facades of the House of the Governor and the west building of the Nunnery are breathtaking examples of thousands of stones fitted into a panorama of geometric, serpentine, supernatural, and human figures. These designs were not simply decorative—all carried religious and cultural connotations. Jeff Kowalski has demonstrated that the latticework represents the "mat" of dynastic authority; the masks in panels epitomize the Yucatec Rain God, Chac, and other supernatural beings; the step-fret is a symbol of the power of the elite class; and the ruler himself is displayed in stone.

The artistic skill employed in the design and aesthetic placement of the buildings and the beauty and intricacy of the stone facades show a mixing of southern Classic Maya forms, Puuc and Chenes motifs, and some Mexican-influenced art. All these elements blend together to make Uxmal one of the most beautiful and interesting of all Mesoamerican ancient cities.

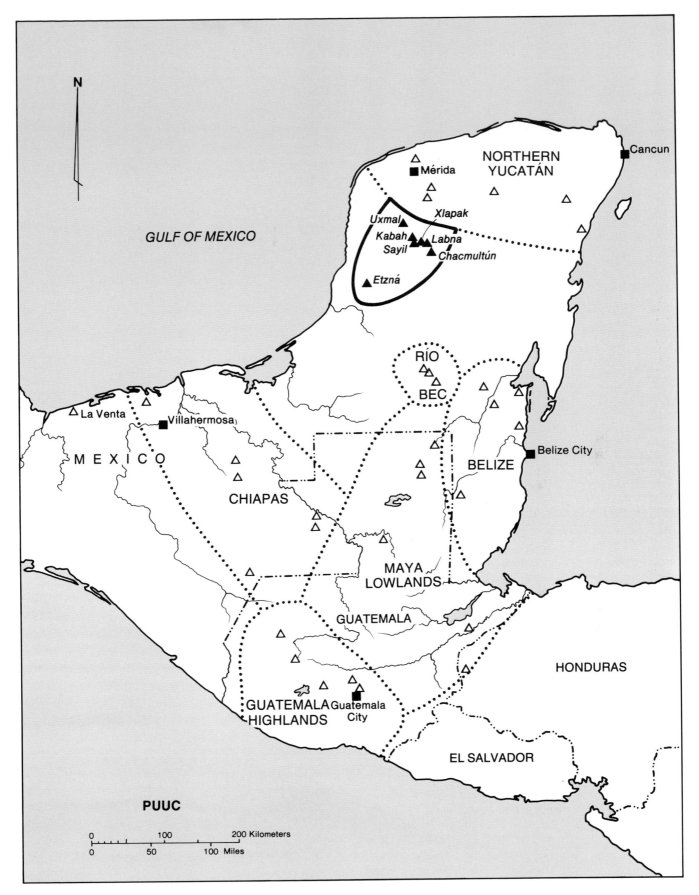

N

NORTHERN
YUCATÁN

Cancun

Mérida

GULF OF MEXICO

Xlapak
Uxmal
Kabah   Labna
Sayil
Chacmultún

Etzná

RÍO

BEC

La Venta

Villahermosa

M E X I C O

Belize City

CHIAPAS

BELIZE

MAYA
LOWLANDS

GUATEMALA

HONDURAS

GUATEMALA
HIGHLANDS

Guatemala
City

EL SALVADOR

PUUC

0   100   200 Kilometers

0   50   100 Miles

Map of the Puuc region in the hills south of Mérida, Mexico.

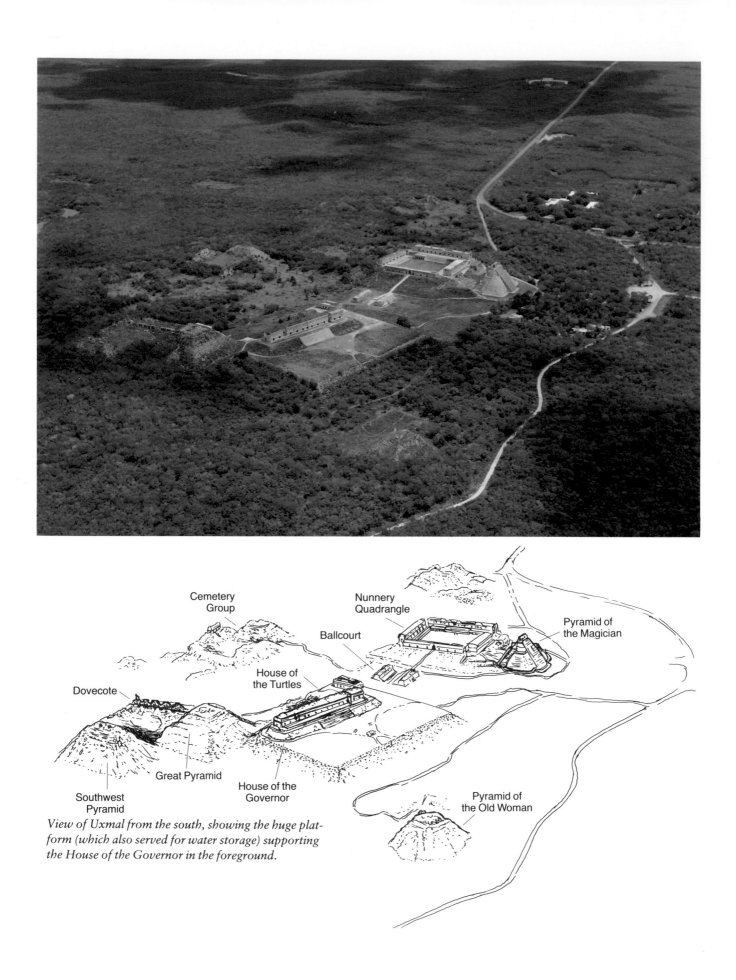

View of Uxmal from the south, showing the huge platform (which also served for water storage) supporting the House of the Governor in the foreground.

*Uxmal from the north with the Pyramid of the Magician and Nunnery Quadrangle
on a line with the ballcourt, House of the Governor, and the Great Pyramid.*

Above: Uxmal. Two of the most beautifully restored Pre-columbian buildings are the Chenes-style Temple of the Magician, built surmounting a graceful curved-wall pyramid, and the Nunnery—four buildings that form a quadrangle.

Below: The Nunnery, inappropriately named by the Spaniards, sits in front (on the west side) of the frequently rebuilt Pyramid of the Magician. According to legend, a dwarf built the pyramid in one night—a feat that inspired its name.

Above: On the east side of the Uxmal ruins stand the House of the Governor, one of the finest and probably the last achievement of the Uxmal Maya, and to its right, the Nunnery and the House of the Magician. Below: The series of standing roof combs inspired the name Dovecote. These standing walls are all that remains of one of the oldest Uxmal buildings, erected between A.D. 700 and 800.

The West Building of the Nunnery was the last constructed in the quadrangle. Its frieze is one of the most spectacular in Mesoamerica.

A close-up look at the detail in Uxmal's Nunnery West Building reveals the intricacies in the workmanship of carving and fitting stone pieces. Here displayed are a stack of masks, beautiful latticework, entwined serpents, and an in place human figure.

Above: This unusual, oval-shaped pyramid was rebuilt at least five times. The oldest, Temple I, which is visible at ground level, was probably constructed in the A.D. 500s. The Chenes Temple IV appears at the top of the main stairway. The House of the Magician (Temple V) tops the pyramid. Temples II and III were covered during rebuilding. Below: One of the two hieroglyphic rings from the ballcourt indicates construction around 900 and may refer to Lord Chac, king of Uxmal. The court is aligned on a north-south axis between the Nunnery Quadrangle and the platform of the House of the Governor.

The Palace at Kabah is a long, range-type building standing atop a rubble-filled platform with a row of vaulted rooms across its front face, producing what appeared to be a two-storied building.

KABAH

Kabah, about 60 miles south of Mérida, is another in the string of visitable Maya sites built in the Puuc Hills. The ruin is bisected by the Mérida to Campeche highway. The buildings include the Codz Poop (Palace of the Masks) with its excessively ornate facade of long-nosed Chac or Sky Serpent masks, a long pyramid platform, and the Palace group on the east side of the road, with the Great Pyramid and Arch to the west.

Although earlier occupations may have stretched back to the late Preclassic, the visible constructions date between A.D. 850 and 900. Kabah was abandoned during the 900s. Only a small portion of the original city has been cleared and stabilized. Kabah was a Puuc-style city—probably with more than 20,000 inhabitants—that may have been connected with Uxmal, 12 miles to the north, by a *sacbe* (Maya road). An extant arch and a portion of a *sacbe* survive at Kabah and another arch was previously reported, but now lost, at Uxmal. Kabah was closely connected politically with Uxmal, for recent discoveries have shown inscriptions at Kabah presenting the name of Lord Chac who ruled Uxmal around A.D. 900.

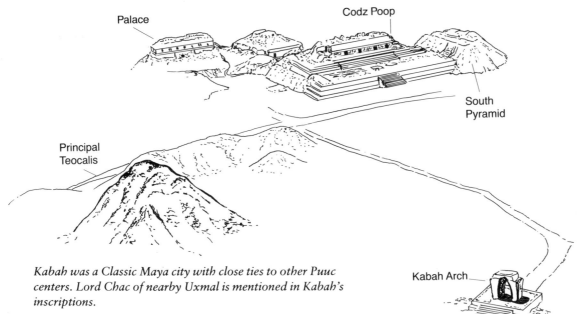

Palace

Codz Poop

South
Pyramid

Principal
Teocalis

Kabah was a Classic Maya city with close ties to other Puuc centers. Lord Chac of nearby Uxmal is mentioned in Kabah's inscriptions.

Kabah Arch

Above: The Kabah Palace group sits on the east side of Highway 261. The central building facing the great platform is the Codz Poop. On the south (right) stands the ceremonial pyramid. These structures date from the late A.D. 800s.

Below: The graceful Arch of Kabah probably marked the entrance to a sacbe (white road) that extended to Uxmal about 12 miles to the north.

Above: The facade of the palace building, Codz Poop, was once covered with about 250 curved-nosed deity masks probably representing the Rain God, Chac; many of the masks are still in place. Left: Stylized masks of Chac cover the facade of the Codz Poop at Kabah.

This beautiful three-story building at Sayil represents the culmination of Puuc Maya architecture. Each story is recessed from the one below. The west (left) side of the Palace has six openings: two doors and four porticoed chambers, each with round columns.

SAYIL, XLAPAK, AND LABNÁ

These three treasures of Puuc Maya architecture are nestled in the forested Puuc hills south of Mérida. From Uxmal in the northwest, exciting late Classic ruins may be found at Kabáh, Sayil, Xlapak, Labná, and Chacmultún. In 1978 the Camino Zona Puuc, a beautiful paved road, was built to make Sayil, Xlapak, and Labná easily accessible to tourists. The new road connects Highway 261 near Kabáh with Oxkutzcab to the east. Chacmultún is near Tekax, a few miles south of Oxkutzcab.

At Sayil, the Palace is the centerpiece of a site containing several hundred structures, although only a few have been excavated. In this region the jungle covers hundreds, perhaps thousands, of mounds hiding buildings built by the Maya. Caan-Cruz and Sabacche are two virtually unknown Puuc sites very near Labná. From the air many mounds can be seen, but the thick undergrowth makes it impossible to determine whether they are natural or cover ancient buildings.

John Lloyd Stephens visited Kabáh in the 1840s and reported that all the ruins scattered about the country were known to the Indians under the general name of *Xlap-pahk*, which means "old walls." Now the name Xlapak refers only to the ruins located between Sayil

and Labná. The only excavated building at this site represents a small palace.

Labná's construction dates from about A.D. 850. El Mirador and the beautiful free-standing Portal Arch on the south end of the plaza are connected to the Palace by a raised *sacbe*. The Palace represents the largest multi-room, terraced platform in the Puuc region. The rubble-filled terrace from which the Palace rises extends some 550 feet; the Palace itself measures about 440 feet in length and 65 feet in height and houses a built-in *chultun* on the second story. There are at least 60 *chultunes* in the Labná area.

These magnificent Puuc Maya cities display the final phase of Classic Maya architecture in all of Maya-land, embodying long graceful buildings decorated with artistically carved stone facades, Greek-like columns, and temple-crowned pyramids. Old Chichén Itzá contains much Puuc style architecture, but subjugation by the Mexicans (Toltecs) caused the delicate Puuc Maya architecture to be superseded by the severe, militaristic, death-oriented buildings of the Postclassic. Although the Classic burgeoning ended in the middle 900s, these cities probably were occupied into the Postclassic and were not abandoned until close to 1100.

The Palace at Sayil is not one large building with interior rooms throughout but rather a loaf-shaped rubble pile with a facade of small rooms that extend only a few yards back into the pyramid.

Sayil's columns, like those of Classic Greece, bulge slightly in the center and are topped by square capitals holding stone lintels.

El Mirador at Sayil lies about one-quarter of a mile from the Palace and is connected with it by a sacbe.

Above: This graceful little Puuc-style building at Xlapak lies between Sayil and Labná. Only a single structure has been restored—a one-story building supporting several mask towers. Right: The hook-nosed god decorating the restored building at Xlapak is often identified as Chac, but possibly represents the Sky Serpent. The curled nose is flanked by square eyes and square ears with attached pendants. The Xlapak building is decorated in Puuc style: an undecorated lower portion, a medial molding made up of colonettes, and a step-fret upper facade topped with a colonette molding that is bounded on the corners by mask towers.

Labná is another beautiful late Maya Classic site nestled in the Puuc Hills of the Yucatán. The excavated portion reveals a huge palace on the north (left), fronted by a plaza crossed by a sacbe *to join El Mirador and the magnificent Portal Arch of Labná on the south.*

Left: This delicate and famous Puuc-style arch (more accurately described as a portal vault) led from a small courtyard beyond to El Mirador. It belongs to a group of buildings from which a ceremonial way extended across the plaza to the Palace. The facade on this side of the arch is decorated with latticework, step-frets, colonettes, and a roof comb.

The Labná arch is an architectural jewel that displays two beautiful thatched Maya huts carved in stone. Below and on the sides of the huts are lattice designs. The lattice and step-fret motifs represent the "mat," symbol of royal authority. A high corbelled arch makes up the portal.

The artificial platform at Labná extends some 550 feet east to west, and the Palace, which sits on it, is about 440 feet long and 65 feet high. The round, white circle is the top of a chultun (cistern) built into the Palace for water storage.

Above: Labná's El Mirador temple supports a roof comb that originally displayed a large seated figure in stucco relief. It is the only temple built on the city's central plaza and demonstrates a break from the design of earlier Classic Maya sites where the ceremonial center of the city contained numerous temples. The magnificent Portal Arch stands next to the pyramid. Right: The Palace facade at Labná displays a wide range of ornate decoration. A human head looking out from the gaping jaws of a reptile, probably a crocodile, is a common Puuc Maya motif.

Cabalpak is a building with six portals on the lower level divided by a stairway leading to the roof. Two additional levels are built against the hill and the fourth level sits on the hilltop.

CHACMULTÚN

As Joyce Kelly observes in her fine *Complete Visitor's Guide to Mesoamerican Ruins*: "Chacmultún is a real sleeper. . . . The site has been known for some time and is not difficult to reach, yet it attracts few visitors." Chacmultún is located in the Puuc Hills east of Labná about 6 miles by dirt road from the modern-day Mexican village of Tekax. It expresses the same Puuc style as Sayil and Labná with which it was contemporaneous.

Three portions of the ancient city have been partially excavated: Cabalpak, a single-storied palace building on the lowest of four man-made terraces—each exhibiting as yet unexcavated buildings—that ascend the hill to the south; the Xetpol group on the east; and the huge Chacmultún group on the west. These three building groups were constructed on the rim of a natural bowl that is about 500 feet across and formed by some of the Puuc Hills. The designs of the Cabalpak and Xetpol buildings follow the pattern of Sayil and Labná, but the facades are much less elaborate than those of Uxmal or Kabáh and the cornice moldings contain no masks and no stone mosaics. The lower facades consist of plain masonry as far up as the medial molding above which are courses of colonettes (small columns). Chacmultún group architecture is a bit more elaborate than that at Cabalpak and Xetpol; Chacmultún has columns, capitals, and a second-story facade decorated with rows of colonettes, columned doorways, and a simulated hut in stone that emulates the Maya thatched-roof huts seen today all over Yucatán. Chacmultún is especially inspiring because its position, tucked away in the Puuc Hills, promotes feelings of solemnity and remoteness associated with a newly discovered ancient ruin.

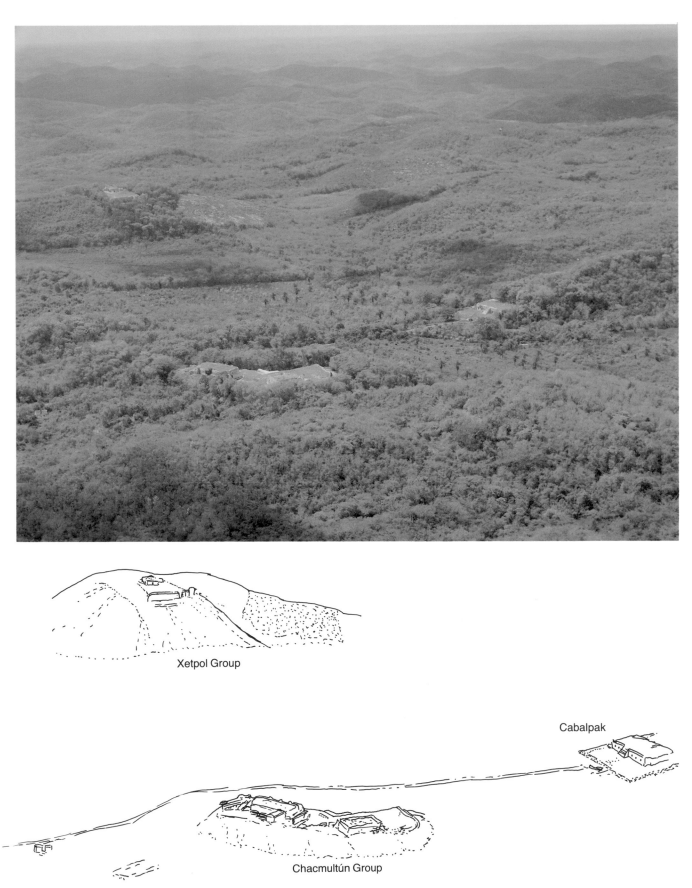

Xetpol Group

Cabalpak

Chacmultún Group

Three partially excavated buildings surrounding a small valley make up the ruins of Chacmultún, a Puuc site near and closely associated with Sayil and Labná. This view from the west *shows the Chacmultún group in the foreground, Cabalpak to the right, and the Xetpol group across the valley.*

Building 4 of the Xetpol group at Chacmultún sits on a hill about 100 feet above the valley. The building is well preserved and contains some remains of wall paintings.

This partially excavated lower-level portion of Cabalpak sits at valley level facing north.

The Chacmultún group, consisting of three large structures, crowns the hill on the west side of the ruin. In the foreground is Building 3 built into the hillside. Building 1, displaying the Doric-type columns, sits on top of an artificial fill.

The Chacmultún group crowns an acropolis on the west side of the valley. Building 3 is fitted into the terrace on the lower level and Buildings 1 and 2 were erected on the top.

Etzná's elevated man-made main plaza is dominated by the Temple of Five Stories, or Templo Mayor, with temples flanking both north and south sides in the style of Maya cities in the Petén. This Maya site has very early roots, but the extant ruins are late Classic. The dates of discovered inscriptions range from A.D. 633 to 810.

ETZNÁ

Etzná (or Edzná), near the busy Gulf Coast city of Campeche, marks the southernmost Puuc-style Maya ruin. Etzná's roots go deep into the past since the system of canals and reservoirs that served the city are known to have been built during Preclassic times. Etzná's inscription dates range from A.D. 633 to 810. Its architecture fits the early Puuc style, and the existing buildings probably date from the late 700s. By the late Classic, Etzná was a sizable city that flourished into the 900s.

The Main Acropolis dominated by the Temple of Five Stories, one of the most striking edifices in Mesoamerica, constituted the ceremonial center of the city and covered an area of some 4,000 square feet. A residential zone joined the acropolis and covered a much larger area. Surrounded by hills, the ruin sits in an oval basin about 9 miles from east to west and 12 miles from north to south.

A system of reservoirs not only furnished water for domestic use but may also have been connected to raised fields where food was grown for the city. The settlement pattern of Etzná resembles that of Dzibilchaltún, which covers some 30 square miles.

Etzná is a showcase of restoration conducted by the National Institute of Anthropology and History of Mexico. During 1987, hundreds of refugees to Mexico from the south were employed to work in the further restoration of Etzná. The Temple of Five Stories, composed of five layered platforms surmounted by a temple bearing a tall roof comb, faces west and sits to the rear (east) of the huge Main Acropolis. Other temples, some partially restored, flanked the acropolis court on the north and south, and a grand stairway provided access to the ceremonial complex. To the west of the Main Acropolis, which supports the Temple of the Five Stories and its adjoining buildings, the Great Plaza has been cleared and largely restored. The Nohol-na with a magnificent entrance stairway stretched across the entire length of the west side of the Great Plaza. The staircase, which may well have served as a grandstand, and a series of short pillars along its top, have been restored.

The South Temple, a five-tiered building with a broad entrance stairway and a top-level temple, that closes off the Great Plaza on the south side, has been excavated and rebuilt along with the ballcourt that adjoins it. Work is also being done on some residential buildings on the north side of the Great Plaza and to the south of the acropolis.

Above: Etzná's Temple of Five Stories. Below: This aerial view from the northwest displays the platform of the Temple of Five Stories. From this angle, the amount of man-made fill needed to create the base upon which the temple-pyramids are con- *structed can be seen together with the grand stairway leading from the main plaza to the pyramid plaza. Since this aerial photograph was taken, the buildings surrounding the plaza to the right (west) of the temple platform have been excavated.*

Above: Closing off the south end of the plaza at Etzná, the Maya built a five-tiered pyramid faced by a wide stairway and topped by a temple. A ballcourt adjoins the temple-pyramid on the east side. Below: The recently excavated building (Nohol-na) with a grandstand-type stairway runs along the west side of the plaza. This is a view from the Temple of Five Stories.

CHAPTER NINE

The Maya of Northern Yucatán

Northern Yucatán and the adjoining Puuc Hills offer the visitor a number of interesting and exciting Maya ruins topped by Chichén Itzá and Uxmal. This region participated equally in the development of Maya culture with the Maya lowlands to the south, and here the Maya Indians still live and cling to the ways of their ancient ancestors.

Maya ruins on the plain of the Yucatán Peninsula, north of the Puuc Hills, range in age from Preclassic to Colonial times. Here the modern-day Yucatec Maya women still wear the ancient *huipiles*, a white, one-piece dress made like a sack and embroidered around the square-cut neck. The men farm their *milpas* with the same slash-and-burn methods practiced by their ancestors 3,000 years ago. These fiercely independent Maya have fought each other, the Spaniards, and the Mexican Federales to maintain their culture and way of life.

The land appears flat although its surface of basal limestone is very rough and pockmarked. The soil is usually not more than a few inches thick and the trees are small. So thick is the undergrowth in much of the Yucatán Peninsula that dozens, if not hundreds, of ancient Maya pyramids and temples may yet be undiscovered. Río Bec B to the south was lost for years after its initial discovery despite concentrated efforts to find it and the fact that its location was known within a few miles. There are virtually no roads and very few trails through the underbrush. The northern plain is dry; there is little rainfall and the only sources of water, except for a few shallow lakes, are large natural wells or *cenotes*. The most famous of these is the *cenote* at Chichén Itzá.

These wells occur where the underlying limestone of the Yucatán north plain has collapsed, exposing the subterranean water table. Because this part of the Yucatán has no surface water, ancient settlements grew up around these wells.

Near the Spanish colonial city of Mérida are several interesting, partially restored ruins. Dzibilchaltún, north of Mérida, is a huge site with origins as far back as 1200 B.C. Its golden age developed in the late Classic, and it was still occupied when the Spaniards arrived. Mayapán and Acancéh lie to the southeast of Mérida. Mayapán was founded around A.D. 1244—a Postclassic city with no earlier beginnings—and for a time served as the capital of all Yucatán. The main pyramid at Acancéh, part of an early Classic Maya city, sits on the north side of a typical Mexican village plaza.

The pride of the Yucatán is Chichén Itzá, long a world-famous tourist attraction. It has been well excavated and there are fine accommodations for visitors. The old Mérida highway once divided the ruins with the generally Classic Maya city to the south and the Postclassic Toltec buildings (mirroring Tula in the Mexican highlands) to the north.

On the east side of the Yucatán Peninsula, in Quintana Roo, Cancun has become a major tourist mecca of posh hostelries created by the Mexican government. Here people from all over the world congregate to swim, play golf, and bask in the warm sunshine. While at Cancun, tourists sometimes visit Chichén Itzá, but more often venture south along the Caribbean coast to visit little Tulum, a Maya outpost village that was still occupied when the Spaniards first cruised the coast. Not far from Tulum lies Cobá a sprawling late Preclassic–Classic Maya ruin between two shallow lakes: Cobá and Macanxoc. In Classic times, Cobá contained twenty or more courtyards and formed the hub of ancient roads (*sacbeob*), one of which extended to Yaxuna some 62 miles west. R.E.W. Adams feels these roads were designed to bring produce into the city from outlying regions. They are called "white roads" because their whitish surfaces made them usable at night when it was cooler to travel. These roads provided a level passage over otherwise rough terrain. Cobá was possibly the largest Classic city in Yucatán after its late Preclassic beginnings.

DZIBILCHALTÚN

Dzibilchaltún endured for almost 3,000 years. Its pre-Maya beginnings go back to 1200–800 B.C. and its Preclassic Maya roots extend to about 500 B.C. The site was still occupied at the time of the Spanish conquest in the early 1500s.

Some 20,000 stone structures have been identified in an area of roughly 30 square miles around the core of the city. About 8,500 of these structures lie within a central zone of about 12 square miles. Of these, nearly three-quarters represent house mounds, which suggests that during its peak occupation in the late Classic and early Postclassic (A.D. 600–1000), the city may have housed 40,000 to 50,000 people, making it one of the larger Precolumbian Maya cities. Major construction appears to have ceased after 1000.

The central area focused around an east-west *sacbe* about a mile and a half long. Parts of this raised roadway were 60 feet wide and 8 feet high. Pyramids, palaces, and ceremonial buildings were built along its course in much the same way as along the Avenue of the Dead at Teotihuacán. A large, double quadrangle of buildings surrounded the sacrificial *cenote*.

The only significant restoration at Dzibilchaltún has been on the Temple of the Seven Dolls at the east end of the *sacbe* and on the Structure 38 platform and temple near the center of the ruin. Additional excavations were begun in the main plaza buildings in 1987.

Dzibilchaltún is important because it was one of the few Precolumbian cities to be more or less continuously occupied from Preclassic times to the beginning of the Colonial period. In addition, it was a sizable city for much of that time. In this respect it compares to Monte Albán, Tikal, and Teotihuacán. However, none of them can boast Dzibilchaltún's long, continuous span of occupancy.

Dzibilchaltun's sacred cenote.

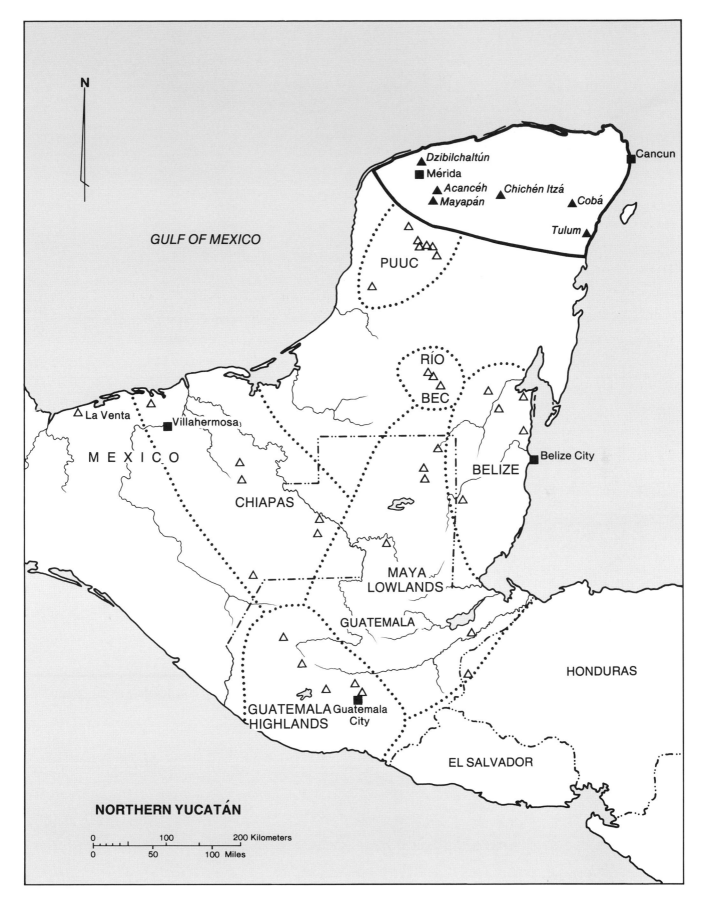

N

GULF OF MEXICO

▲ Dzibilchaltún
■ Mérida
▲ Acancéh   ■ Cancun
▲ Mayapán   ▲ Chichén Itzá
              ▲ Cobá
△ △ △   ▲ Tulum
△ △ △

PUUC

△

RÍO

△
△
BEC

△ La Venta   △
■ Villahermosa   △

M E X I C O   ■ Belize City

△   BELIZE
△   △

CHIAPAS

△
△   MAYA
         LOWLANDS
△

         GUATEMALA

△

HONDURAS

△
△   ■ Guatemala
GUATEMALA   City
HIGHLANDS

EL SALVADOR

NORTHERN YUCATÁN

0   100   200 Kilometers
0   50   100 Miles

Maya sites of the north Yucatán Peninsula.

Dzibilchaltún from the west. In the foreground is the sacred cenote *Xlacah—100 feet across and 140 feet deep—revered by the ancient Maya who surrounded it with a double quadrangle of buildings. A small chapel built by the Spaniards in the 1590s may be seen in the plaza to the side of the* cenote. *The path follows an ancient* sacbe *(causeway) eastward to the Temple of the Seven Dolls.*

*At the east end of the partially restored center of Dzibilchaltún is a platform
supporting a stela, ruins of three buildings belonging to the Seven Dolls complex,
and the Temple of the Seven Dolls.*

Left: From the stela platform along the sacbe (raised roadway) east of Dzibilchaltún's center, one can look directly through two of the four doorways in the Temple of the Seven Dolls. Below: Dzibilchaltún's most famous building is the Temple of the Seven Dolls—a square building with a large vaulted room. Doorways and windows front all four sides. Windows are very unusual in Classic Maya architecture.

This fragment of a Classic age stela was used to line a subfloor passageway in a Postclassic platform along the north side of Dzibilchaltún's central plaza. Reuse of broken older monuments at later times attests to the very long occupation of this northern Yucatán city.

Two sacbeob *crossed at the center of ancient Dzibilchaltún, where the modern paths now intersect. To the right of the Colonial church, the visible trail swings around Pyramid 36 and passes the foundations of Structure 38.*

Above: This early Classic Maya pyramid, four-tiered with apron moldings, closely resembles Uaxactún's famous Preclassic pyramid. Fifteen hundred years ago it faced an open plaza as it now faces the central square of the little Yucatán village of Acancéh. Below: Present-day Maya women attend the village market in the square adjoining an ancient Maya temple-pyramid.

This low colonaded temple lies to the side of Mayapán's El Castillo. A mask of Chac, the Maya Rain God, stares out from the central pair of columns.

MAYAPÁN

At Mayapán the ancient Maya begin to overlap the dim beginnings of post-Conquest history, for the rise and fall of Mayapán occurred within two centuries of the Spanish conquest. These times were remembered in the Indians myths, recollections, and prophecies recorded by Fray Diego de Landa and recalled in the Book of Chilam Balam (see Roys 1967).

According to M. D. Coe, the Itzá were Mexicanized Chontal Maya who had settled near modern Campeche during the time of the Toltec occupation of Chichén Itzá (A.D. 1100s). They seem to have been almost universally despised by the natives of Yucatán who referred to them as tricksters and rascals. Some time around A.D. 1224 or later, the Itzá moved into Chichén Itzá, which had been abandoned earlier by its Toltec leaders. Later (ca. 1244), the Itzá founded Mayapán, one of the last cities to be built by the ancient Maya.

The Itzá king, Kukulcán II, devised an Aztec-like system for supporting Mayapán. By force of arms he had subjugated much of the Yucatán Peninsula, requiring each of the local provinces to pay tribute in food and other goods. To insure compliance with his orders for tribute, Kukulcán II held the provincial rulers and their families hostage at Mayapán. Following Kukulcán II, an Itzá family named Cocom took power, and about 1283 Mayapán became the capital of Yucatán.

Mayapán, located 30 miles from Mérida, was a walled city encompassing some 2.5 square miles and enclosing 2,000 dwellings and second-rate copies of Chichén Itzá's ceremonial buildings. During Mayapán's best times it housed about 12,000 people.

About 1440 the Mexican Maya family of Xiu, joined by the Maya princes, supported a revolt within Mayapán. The Itzá were executed and the city destroyed.

Mayapán does not have the charm and sparkle of Chichén Itzá. Not only did it contain pale imitations of Chichén Itzá's magnificent buildings, but it also has not been so lavishly excavated and restored. It is certainly worth a visit, however, because El Castillo, the great pyramid in the center of the ruin, is impressive even without restoration. Alongside El Castillo lies a *cenote* and the Structure of the Chac Masks. Scattered through the jungle are the ruins of other temples and former elite residences.

Mayapán represented the last gasp of the Postclassic Maya. This photograph shows El Castillo as a much less refined version of the beautiful Castillo at Chichén Itzá. Mayapán was the walled capital of Yucatán for about 200 years until it was destroyed in the early 1400s.

Several of Mayapán's temple platforms sport serpent heads at the tops of the balustrades flanking the staircases. This very late Postclassic construction is crude in comparison with earlier Maya building.

CHICHÉN ITZÁ

Chichén Itzá is the best known of all Mesoamerican ruins, and yet our archaeological knowledge of it is very limited. When it was restored, few records were kept, and it is said the cockroaches ate the markings off the salvaged building stones and artifacts, rendering them virtually useless for detailed study.

During the late Classic, Chichén Itzá was a relatively small Puuc Maya town, probably named Uucil-abnal (Seven Bushes). Elaborately ornamented palace units (now called the Nunnery), small temple pyramids like Red House and House of the Deer, and numerous other buildings surrounded the Caracol—perhaps Mayadom's most sophisticated astronomical observatory. The arrival of more warlike Mexicans, probably Toltecs, catapulted the city into the forefront of Yucatec Maya history.

The history of Chichén Itzá's Classic and Postclassic stages is still very controversial, for there is little hard archaeological evidence to interpret. Even the chronicles written in early historic times contain much folklore, making it difficult to sort fact from legend.

It is now generally accepted that the Chontal (or Putun Itzá) Maya, whose homeland in late Classic times was along the south coast of the Gulf of Mexico, became the dominant trading people of the Yucatán. The trade in cotton cloth, slaves, salt, and honey enriched Chichén Itzá and the cities of the Puuc as important trading centers. The Chontal also traded with highland Mexican cities including Toltec Tula. The Chontal Itzá connection with the cities of the Mexican highlands is the likely source of the Mexican motifs, such as the feathered serpent that appeared in the late Classic at Chichén Itzá and the Puuc cities.

Recent studies by David Kelley, Jeff Kowalski, and others indicate that the Itzá, led by Kakupacal, assumed power in Uucil-abnal (Chichén Itzá) about A.D. 866 or 869. From the Itzá came the name Chichén Itzá (The Mouth of the Well of the Itzá). About 100 years later the Toltecs of Tula, or perhaps the Mexicanized Chontal Maya, either by invitation or force, became the new rulers of Chichén Itzá. In his 1980 version of *The Maya*, M. D. Coe suggests the following scenario. The Toltecs of Tula in central Mexico were torn by dissension between the followers of the deities Quetzalcoatl (Feathered Serpent in the Nahuatl language of the Toltecs) and Tezcatlipoca (Smoking Mirror). The king, Topiltzin Quetzalcoatl, lost and was forced to flee with his supporters, probably about A.D. 987. They crossed the Gulf of Mexico to the coast of Yucatán. Maya sources indicate the arrival in Katun 4 Ahau (which ended in 987) of someone calling himself Kukulcán (Feathered Serpent in the Maya tongue), who ultimately conquered the Maya

of Yucatán and established his capital at Chichén Itzá. The murals in the Temple of the Warriors seem to verify the attack on Yucatán by the Toltecs. Tula-like architecture and stone reliefs now cover the north half of Chichén Itzá: El Castillo, the Temple of the Warriors with columns and flat roofs, chacmools, tzompantlis, Toltec warrior cults, and atlantean Toltec warriors. Postclassic Chichén Itzá resembled Tula but on a grander scale, since all these attributes of construction may be seen at the ruins of Toltec Tula (located about 50 miles north of Mexico City).

Adams suggests there had to have been a cultural relationship between Chichén Itzá and Tula because Chichén Itzá provides a grandiose mirror of Tula.

Kowalski suggests that during the late 800s and early 900s Chichén Itzá and the Puuc cities were competing with each other both economically and politically, which disrupted the Chontal trade in the region with highland Mexico. This induced the Toltecs to bring in military force to stabilize Yucatán by establishing a capital at Chichén Itzá. A more powerful Chichén Itzá probably forced the abandonment of the Puuc cities and ended the Maya Classic stage.

COBÁ

Most of the ruins of Cobá still lie beneath the tangle of jungle. In Classic times the city comprised many elite architectural groups interspersed with hundreds of small houses built near a group of shallow lakes in the forests of Quintana Roo, about 30 miles northwest of Tulum. Three principal pyramids have been partially cleared and stabilized: the Castillo of Group B at Cobá, Conjunto Las Pinturas, and the Castillo at Nohoch Mul. All the structures at Cobá were linked to one another and to other neighboring settlements by a series of sixteen arrow-straight roads, or *sacbeob*. One such road extends about 62 miles westward to Yaxuna, only a few miles from Chichén Itzá. The Maya expended considerable effort to construct these roads throughout their domain, but they had no useful wheel nor beast of burden for the conduct of commerce; nevertheless the roads facilitated the movement of produce over rough and swampy terrain and could be used at night to avoid the sweltering heat of tropical days.

Some archaeologists believe Cobá had direct relationships with the Petén rather than merely exhibiting the Petén's influence like the Río Bec and Puuc cities did. Cobá may actually have been built and inhabited by people from the Petén. It was one of the earliest major sites in northeastern Yucatán. Sylvanus G. Morley dated Stelae 4 and 6 at around 9.9.10.0.0 (A.D. 623). More than twenty of Cobá's stelae date from 623 to 780. There are also indications the Cobá region was occupied into late Postclassic times (1400s).

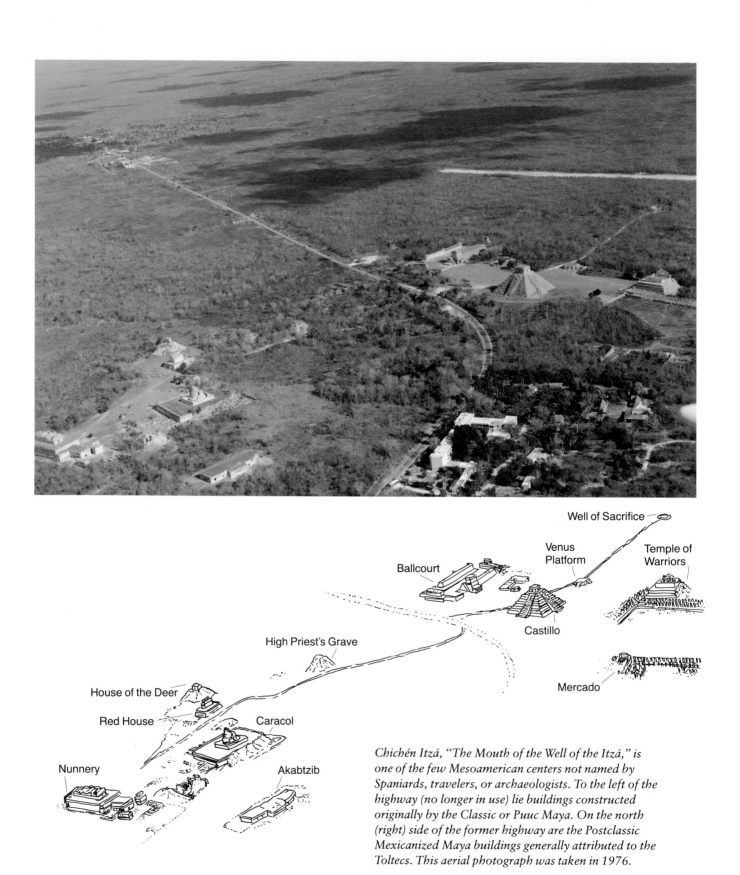

Well of Sacrifice

Venus Platform

Temple of Warriors

Ballcourt

Castillo

High Priest's Grave

Mercado

House of the Deer

Red House

Caracol

Nunnery

Akabtzib

Chichén Itzá, "The Mouth of the Well of the Itzá," is one of the few Mesoamerican centers not named by Spaniards, travelers, or archaeologists. To the left of the highway (no longer in use) lie buildings constructed originally by the Classic or Puuc Maya. On the north (right) side of the former highway are the Postclassic Mexicanized Maya buildings generally attributed to the Toltecs. This aerial photograph was taken in 1976.

*Above: This view of the west end of the Central Plaza from the
north displays El Castillo, the Venus Platform at the mouth of
the trail leading to the Well of Sacrifice, and the ballcourt.
Below: Almost every Precolumbian Mesoamerican site
contains one or more ballcourts. This was one of seven at
Chichén Itzá and one of the largest in Mesoamerica—nearly as
large as a football field. It is Mexican-style with vertical sides
and stone rings. Attesting to the serious ceremonial aspects of
the game is a bas-relief showing the decapitation of the captain
of a losing team.*

Above: The Nunnery complex (foreground), built around A.D. 600, is probably the oldest major structure at Chichén Itzá. At the upper right is the well-known Caracol built upon a late Classic Puuc-style base; the tower has an observatory chamber with openings that reflect the moon's declination, the sun's vernal equinox, and the summer solstice. At the upper left is the Red House.
Right: Postclassic El Castillo, named by Bishop Landa in the seventeenth century, was dedicated to the feathered serpent Kukulcán (Maya for Quetzalcoatl). Visible at the east end of the plaza is the Temple of the Warriors.

Above: For several days before and after both spring and fall equinoxes, the light of the setting sun creates a writhing serpent along the balustrade on the north face of El Castillo. This spectacular and awe-inspiring event is now called the hierophany. This phenomenon is no accident; the architects of ancient Chichén Itzá designed El Castillo to produce this serpent of light. Left: The Red Jaguar Throne belongs to a smaller earlier pyramid that lies beneath El Castillo. A stairway beneath the outer staircase has been excavated upward from ground level to the inner temple where the splendid jade-encrusted Red Jaguar Throne may be seen in place.

The Temple of a Thousand Columns flanks the Pyramid of the Warriors on two sides. This building is amazingly similar to the Great Vestibule at the foot of the Temple of the Atlanteans at Tula. The bas-reliefs carved on the columns indicate the importance of warriors in Postclassic Chichén Itzá—evidence of Toltec influence.

Feathered serpent columns facing the chacmool stand at the portal of the Temple of the Warriors. Two Mexican attributes introduced into Chichén Itzá were the chacmool (a reclining figure with a flat surface on its stomach designed as a receptacle for the hearts of sacrificial victims) and Kukulcán (the Maya name for the feathered serpent deity).

Top: The Caracol (so-named in Spanish for its interior winding staircase) at Classic Chichén Itzá represents the most obvious astronomical observatory in Mayaland. The circular structure stands on top of two broad platforms. Puuc style art decorates the facades of both the observatory and platforms. Below left: The low building attached to the Nunnery (Monjas) platform presents an unusually intense display of Chac masks, both on the corners and wall faces. Virtually no part of the facade has been left unadorned. Below right: The Iglesia at Chichén Itzá is an outstanding example of late Classic Puuc-style architecture and ornamentation. A lower plain wall is capped by an elaborately carved roof vault facade depicting masks of Chac, the Rain God, with his projecting curled nose.

Carved stone images of Kukulcán (Feathered Serpent) support the lintel over the opening to the upper portion of the Temple of the Jaguars on the southeast corner of the ballcourt at Chichén Itzá. The richly dressed human figure on the flanking square column has been rendered in Mexican style.

Above and opposite: This Maya ball-game ritual scene may have reenacted the legend of the Hero Twins' exploits in the underworld. They played the game with the Lords of Xibalba and the loser was decapitated. These center sections of the Maya ballgame ritual scenes appear on opposite sides of the ballcourt. (Drawings by Ethne Barnes). Left: The relief on the east side of Chichén Itzá's ballcourt depicts a beheading scene from which the drawing above is taken.

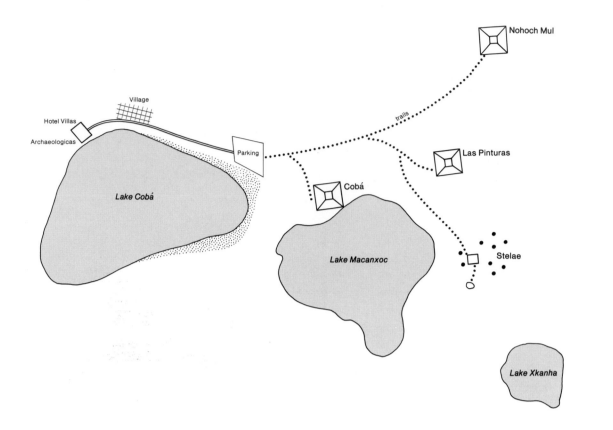

Nohoch Mul

trails

Las Pinturas

Village

Hotel Villas

Archaeologicas

Parking

Lake Cobá

Cobá

Lake Macanxoc

Stelae

Lake Xkanha

COBÁ

| 0 | 1/4 | 1/2 mile |
| 0 | | .8 kilometers |

Lake Zacalpuc

Trail map of the Cobá ruins.

The Postclassic Maya Conjunto Las Pinturas at Cobá consists of a four-tiered pyramid capped by a small temple with traces of a painted mural.

The painted mural on the stone lintel of the Conjunto Las Pinturas temple displays a Postclassic codex style similar to the surviving Maya codices. The paintings contain a Mexican year sign indicating it was done during Mayanized Mexican times at Cobá.

Above: The Castillo faces west toward the main plaza and Lake Macanxoc. This stepped pyramid is 78 feet high, has a rubble core, and in Classic times was finished smooth with plaster. Below: Nohoch Mul is a group of ruins just over one-half mile northeast of the Castillo at Cobá. The pyramid of the Castillo at Nohoch Mul is similar in design and style to Tikal in the Petén, but instead of a majestic temple and roof comb, the Castillo is crowned by an out-of-proportion, flat, little temple in the style of Postclassic Tulum.

Many carved stone stelae are scattered among the trees that now cover the old Maya plaza of Macanxoc at Cobá. This recently reset stela, although badly eroded, displays an unknown ruler and a series of glyph panels.

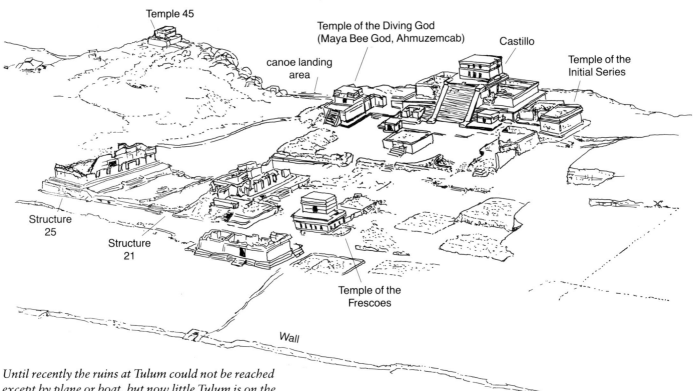

Temple 45

Temple of the Diving God
(Maya Bee God, Ahmuzemcab)

canoe landing
area

Castillo

Temple of the
Initial Series

Structure
25

Structure
21

Temple of the
Frescoes

Wall

*Until recently the ruins at Tulum could not be reached
except by plane or boat, but now little Tulum is on the
international tourist circuit and can be reached by a
hard-surfaced road from Cancun. The walled center,
beautifully situated on a limestone cliff, 40 feet above
the Caribbean Sea, was constructed for the most part
during the A.D. 1400s.*

Tulum was likely "the very large town" seen from the sea by Grijalva and Diaz in 1518 since it was a Postclassic Maya frontier site inhabited at the time of Spanish conquest. The masonry is crude by Classic Maya standards, but the buildings were originally covered with stucco, which gave them a more symmetrical appearance.

TULUM

Tulum was a very late Postclassic village founded during the time of Mayapán dominance. People still lived there when the Spaniards arrived. On May 7, 1518, an expedition led by Juan de Grijalva sailed along the coast of Yucatán and Juan Diaz, a member of the expedition, reported "a city or town so large that Seville would not have seemed more considerable nor better." That city was probably Tulum.

The picturesque setting of Tulum's ruins, located on the spectacular white-beached Caribbean seacoast about 40 miles south of Playa del Carmen, makes it a "must" stop for visitors to Cancun. The ruins stand on the summit of a limestone cliff 40 feet high. The land slopes away from the cliff and then rises again to form a ridge about 600 feet from the cliff. The core of the village (Coe estimates only 500 or 600 inhabitants) was enclosed on three sides by a rectangular wall. The fourth (east) side faces the sea. Tulum means "wall" or "rampart" in the modern Maya language, indicating a historical origin for the name. The ancient Maya name was Zama (dawn).

Archaeological research directed by Arthur Miller has provided mural painting, architectural, and ceramic evidence confirming the first occupation of Tulum at around A.D. 1200. We know that occupation continued because the Temple of the Frescoes and the Temple of the Diving God were not erected until 250 years later. After the Spanish conquest, the site became a ceremonial center for the local Maya Indians until well into the twentieth century.

Tulum's Postclassic masonry seems crude compared to the magnificent constructions of the Classic Maya; yet when the sloppy stonework was covered with white coats of plaster, the city must have appeared impressive to the Spaniards. Tulum was a frontier town, one of a number of small warring states of the Yucatán after Mayapán's domination ended; it was a trading city on the circumpeninsula canoe trade route. Salt from the northern Yucatán coast was a major trade item. Exports from Tulum were honey and beeswax. Honey was Tulum's specialty—certainly as a sweetening agent it was very popular in the days before sugar cane. (Thus, the name Diving God is probably not as appropriate as the Maya Bee God—Ahmuzemcab.) The city may have been governed by merchants who replaced the divine-right kings of earlier times. Ancient pilgrims to the Moon Goddess shrine on Cozumel probably departed from this village.

Arthur Miller suggests the city was constructed by Mayanized Mexicans. M. D. Coe, however, feels later Tulum was Maya, that by the 1400s these people had forgotten the Mexican influences that permeated the Yucatán Peninsula hundreds of years earlier.

Above: Unfortunately, these murals at Tulum are fading.
Goddess Ixchel appears holding the god Chac in each hand
with colorin bean pods behind her. These deities were painted
some time after A.D. 1450. By this time the Maya had shed
much of the Mexican influence and Tulum was a ceremonial
center used by the Maya until well into the twentieth century.

Despite the seemingly sloppy Postclassic masonry, Tulum's
walls were lavishly decorated with painted and carved panels.
The Temple of the Frescoes contains a set of well-preserved,
painted murals inside and a series of once-painted relief
carvings along the facade above the lower level columns.
The Castillo may be seen in the right background.

This temple long referred to as the Temple of the Diving God (but more recently as that of Ahmuzemcab, the Bee God, because Tulum was an exporter of honey) flanks the Castillo on the north. It rests on a small platform with a west-facing stairway. *Right:* This sculpted figure in a niche above the doorway gives the name to the Temple of the Diving God. He has been identified as Ahmuzemcab, the bee, in the act of flying downward. Bee-like features are the fanned tail, wings attached to the arms, and once-painted color markings.

Above: The Castillo was named by John L. Stephens when he visited the site in the 1840s. It was built over an earlier palace-type building. In front of the two-room temple is a sacrificial stone on which victims were extended while their hearts were torn out. Below: Structure 25 lies to the northwest of the Castillo. A polychrome stucco figure of the Bee God is fitted in a niche above the central doorway.

Left: This seated ceramic figure, about 31" tall, in the collection of the British Museum of Mankind is reported to have been recovered from Tulum. It epitomizes Postclassic Maya artistic style. Right: Tulum's Castillo perches near the edge of a 40-foot-high limestone cliff fronting the Caribbean Sea. This cliff provides a barrier to access from the sea except at the small cove and beach just north of the Castillo. In ancient times this cove served as a landing place for the seagoing trading canoes.

Glossary

ACROPOLIS: A raised eminence or platform, either natural or artificial, standing above a city, upon which buildings stand.

ALTAR: A raised platform or structure used in connection with the worship of a deity.

ARCHAEOASTRONOMY: Application of the study of the stars and planets to ancient cultures.

ARCHAEOLOGY: The scientific study of past human life, most often applied to preliterate times.

ART HISTORY: The study of sculpture, glyphic writing, painting, ceramics, and other human artistic creations.

ATLATL: A hand-held stick used as an arm extension for throwing a spear or dart. The word comes from the Aztec language, Nahuatl.

BAKTUN: A period of 400 tuns of 360 days each (slightly less than 400 solar years); part of the Maya method of computing time.

BALLCOURT: A rectangular or I-shaped space, usually with masonry-faced sides, used throughout Mesoamerica for a game played with a rubber ball.

BALUSTRADE: Either side of a stairway.

BAR-AND-DOT NUMERALS: The bar was equal to 5 and the dot equal to 1 in the Mesoamerican recording of numbers.

BASAL PLATFORM: A raised, horizontal, flat surface that acts as a base for structures.

BAS-RELIEF: Sculpture in low relief having only a small projection from the background.

BATTER: The sloping face of a wall when viewed in cross section. A wall with inverted taper (thicker at the top than at the bottom) has negative batter.

BEARING WALL: A material layer, usually of masonry construction, that encloses space and carries the thrust of the roof load to the ground or substructure.

CALENDAR ROUND: The 52-year period at the end of which the Maya calendar begins to repeat itself with day names and designators.

CASTILLO: A Spanish word for "castle" applied erroneously to the principal pyramid at many Mesoamerican sites.

CENOTE: A natural well in a collapsed portion of the surface limestone in the Yucatán.

CHAC: Maya god of rain.

CHACMOOL: Reclining stone figure of Toltec origin found at Tula and Chichén Itzá; a receptacle is carved over the abdomen to hold sacrificial hearts.

CHENES-STYLE ARCHITECTURE: Characteristic style of Yucatán, employing doorways framed by huge monster masks and facades of step-frets, lattice work, and stacked masks.

CHULTUN: An artificial cistern for collection of rainwater.

CODEX (PL. CODICES): Prehispanic books of folded deerskin or bark paper made by the Maya, Mixtecs, Aztecs, and others; written in glyphic or pictographic form.

CORBEL VAULT: A ceiling vault in the form of an inverted V, constructed by edging successively higher rows of stones over the open space until a single row of capstones can bridge the remaining space; the Mesoamerican substitute for the arch.

CORNICE: A projection that crowns a building or wall.

CULTURE: The sum of nonbiological beliefs, attainments, traditions, customs, mores, and methods of providing food, clothing, and shelter in the life-style of any group of people. These essentials are modified and passed along from generation to generation.

CYCLE: In the Precolumbian calendar, any of many repeating series of calendrical-religious phenomena, such as the 52-year Calendar Round or solar or lunar cycle.

DANZANTES: So-called "dancers," bas-reliefs at Monte Albán, probably representing captives of early rulers.

ELITE: A portion of society treated as socially superior with special privileges, luxury goods, responsibilities, and accommodations—a ruling class.

ETHNOLOGY: The study of contemporary human cultures.

FACADE: The facing of a wall or building often decorated and emphasized architecturally.

FEATHERED SERPENT: The ubiquitous mythical serpent with feathers found in Precolumbian America from the southwest United States to Central America. As a deity it bears such names as Quetzalcoatl and Kukulcán.

FRET(FRETWORK): Ornamental design in painting or in relief on stone consisting of continuous running lines in short, straight segments. It may also be painted on pottery.

FRESCO: Painting on freshly spread plaster before it dries.

FRIEZE: A sculptured or ornamented band.

GALLERY: A roofed promenade; a long narrow passage.

GLYPH: A carved or painted figure or character, incised or in relief; a hieroglyph.

HERO TWINS: Hunahpu and Xbalanque, who overcame the lords of the underworld in the *Popul Vuh*.

HIEROPHANY: A word describing the serpent-in-light phenomenon that appears at sunset on El Castillo at Chichén Itzá during the times of the two equinoxes.

HOTUN: A period of 10 years; one half a katun.

ICONOGRAPHY: The study of the art of representation by pictures or images.

INCISE: To cut into shallowly, to inscribe.

KATUN: A period of 20 tuns (7,200 days) or slightly less than 20 years.

KIN: A day in the Maya calendar.

KUKULCÁN: The Maya name for the god Quezalcoatl, the feathered serpent.

LINGUISTICS: The study of languages.

LINTEL: A horizontal load-bearing member of wood or stone spanning the opening in a doorway or window.

LONG COUNT: The complete expression of a date in the Maya calendar in baktuns (roughly 400 years), katuns (roughly 20 solar years), tuns (360 days), uinals (20 days), and kin (1 day) from the base date of the Maya era, August 11, 3114 B.C.

LOW RELIEF: Sculpture having only a slight projection; the same as bas-relief.

MANO: The mano was the hand grinding stone drawn back and forth across the metate, or fixed stone receptacle, with a concave upper surface. Corn was placed on the metate and ground with the mano.

MARKET: A place in a village, town, or city where goods and produce are sold and exchanged.

METATE: See Mano.

MILPA: A small, burned clearing in the forest, planted and abandoned after a few years; a part of the slash-and-burn agricultural system.

PALACE: A place of elite residence.

PETÉN: The department (province) encompassing the lowlands in northern Guatemala.

PLATFORM: A level fill of rubble used as a base for the construction of buildings or pyramids.

PLAZA: A planned, open space surrounded or partially surrounded by structures.

POCHTECA: Aztec merchants who traveled long distances and traded exotic products throughout Mesoamerica.

POST-AND-LINTEL CONSTRUCTION: Architectural technique based upon vertical pillars or posts spanned by horizontal lintels.

PORTICO: A porch with a roof supported by columns.

PUUC: A late Classic Maya culture named for the low range of limestone hills in western Yucatán.

PYRAMID-PLAZA: Maya ceremonial construction of a temple group consisting of an open plaza surrounded, generally on three sides, by temple-pyramids.

QUETZAL: A Central American bird of brilliant plumage much prized by the Maya.

QUETZALCOATL: Feathered serpent deity of the Aztecs and their predecessors, known as Kukulcán to the Maya.

RANGE-STYLE BUILDING: A row of connected rooms forming a long, generally single-story, building.

RESTORATION: The process of reassembling the fallen parts of ancient structures into their presumed original condition.

ROOF COMB: A structure placed on the roof of a building, which resembles the comb of a cock; very often open work.

RUBBLE: Rough, broken stones used in filling courses in walls, building platforms, and pyramids.

SACBE (PL. SACBEOB): A raised artificial road built by the Maya.

SARCOPHAGUS: A stone coffin.

SEPULCHRE: A place of burial, a tomb.

STABILIZATION: The process of partially rebuilding existing portions of ancient structures for purposes of preservation.

STAGE: A degree or level of cultural development.

STELA (PL. STELAE): A freestanding stone monument, usually sculpted.

STUCCO: A limestone plaster in a plastic state used to form a hard cover over masonry or to be worked into sculptured forms.

STYLE: The characteristics of an object, structure, or thing that brings it within a recognized fashion or mode; examples are ceramics, architecture, sculpture, or painting.

TALUD-TABLERO: A Classic Teotihuacán architectural feature composed of a vertical, rectangular panel (*tablero*) cantilevered over a sloping wall (*talud*).

TEMPLE-PYRAMID: A rubble-filled and masonry-faced pyramid topped by a masonry temple.

TUN: Maya term for "year" usually applied to the period of 360 days.

TZOMPANTLI: A rack or platform on which the skulls of sacrificial victims were displayed.

UINAL: The Maya "month" of 20 days.

VAULT: An arched structure usually forming a ceiling or roof.

VENEER: To overlay a rubble substructure with a masonry facing or coating.

WATTLE-AND-DAUB CONSTRUCTION: A method of constructing buildings in which walls are made of upright poles interwoven with small branches and plastered with mud.

WERE-JAGUAR: A creature resulting from the mythical mating of a human and a jaguar.

XIBALBA: Maya underworld.

Bibliography

Adams, R.E.W.
1977   *Prehistoric Mesoamerica*. Little Brown and Company, Boston.
1986   "Archaeologists Explore Guatemala's Lost City of the Maya, Río Azul." *National Geographic*, Vol. 169, No. 4, April 1986, 420–450.

Ashmore, Wendy (ed)
1981   *Lowland Maya Settlement Patterns*. School of American Research, University of New Mexico Press, Albuquerque.

Aveni, Anthony F.
1977   *Native American Astronomy*. University of Texas Press, Austin.

Ball, Joseph W.
1980   "The Archaeological Ceramics of Chinkultic, Chiapas, Mexico." *Papers of the New World Archaeological Foundation, No. 43*. NWAF, Brigham Young University, Provo Utah.

Bardsley, Sandy
1989   "Copán: A Compilation of Known and Tentative Data." *U Mut Maya*, Tom Jones and Carolyn Young, Eds. Arcata, CA.

Bernal, Ignacio.
1969   *The Olmec World*. Translated by Doris Heyden and Fernando Horcasitas. University of California Press, Berkeley.
1975   *Mexico Before Cortez*. Anchor Books, New York.

Blanton, Richard E., Stephen A. Kowalewski, Gary Feinman, and Jill Appel
1981   *Ancient Mesoamerica*. Cambridge University Press, Cambridge.

Bricker, Victoria R., and Jeremy A. Sabloff, (eds)
1981   *Supplement to the Handbook of Middle American Indians*, vol. 1: *Archaeology*. University of Texas Press, Austin.

Caso, Alfonso
1958   *The Aztecs, People of the Sun*. University of Oklahoma Press, Norman.

Cervantes, Maria Antonieta
1978   *Treasures of Ancient Mexico from the National Anthropological Museum*. 2d ed. Crescent Books, New York.

Coe, M. D.
1980   *The Maya*. Rev. ed. Thames and Hudson, London.
1984   *Mexico*. 3d ed. Thames and Hudson, London.

Coe, M. D., and Richard A. Diehl
1980   *In the Land of the Olmec*. 2 vols. University of Texas Press, Austin.

Coe, William R.
1967   *Tikal: A Handbook of the Ancient Maya Ruins*. University Museum, University of Pennsylvania, Philadelphia.

Dias del Castillo, Bernal
1966   *The True History of the Conquest of New Spain*. Translated by A. P. Maudslay. London, 1908–1916. American edition; H. Wolff, New York.

Diehl, Richard A.
1983   *Tula, the Toltec Capital of Ancient Mexico*. Thames and Hudson, London.

Edmonson, Munro S.
1971   *The Book of Counsel: The Popol Vuh of the Quiche Maya of Guatemala*. Middle American Research Institute, Publ. 35. Tulane University, New Orleans.

Ferguson, William M., and John Q. Royce
1979   *Maya Ruins of Mexico in Color*. University of Oklahoma Press, Norman.
1984   *Maya Ruins in Central America in Color*. University of New Mexico Press, Albuquerque.

Grove, David C.
1984   *Chalcatzingo Excavations on the Olmec Frontier.*
        Thames and Hudson, London.

Hammond, Norman
1982   *Ancient Maya Civilization.* Rutgers University Press,
        New Brunswick, N.J.
1986   "New Light on the Most Ancient Maya." *Man* Vol.
        21(3), pp. 399–413.

Hammond, Norman (ed)
1974   *Mesoamerican Archaeology, New Approaches.* Uni-
        versity of Texas Press, Austin.

Henderson, John S.
1981   *The World of the Ancient Maya.* Cornell University
        Press, Ithaca.

Heyden, Doris, and Paul Gendrop
1975   *Pre-Columbian Architecture in Mesoamerica.* Harry
        N. Abrams, New York.

Horcasitas, Fernando
1979   *The Aztecs, Then and Now.* Ocelot, Mexico City.

Hunter, C. Bruce
1977   *A Guide to Ancient Mexican Ruins.* University of
        Oklahoma Press, Norman.

Kelley, David H.
1976   *Deciphering the Maya Script.* University of Texas
        Press, Austin.

Kelley, Joyce
1982   *The Complete Visitor's Guide to Mesoamerican
        Ruins.* University of Oklahoma Press, Norman.

King, Jaime Litvak
1985   *Ancient Mexico, An Overview.* University of New
        Mexico Press, Albuquerque.

Kowalski, Jeff Karl
1987   *The House of the Governor.* University of
        Oklahoma Press, Norman.

Kubler, George A.
1975   *The Art and Architecture of Ancient America.* 2d
        rev. ed. Penguin Books, New York.

Maudslay, Alfred P.
1889–   *Biiologia Centrali-Americana.* 5 vols. Porter,
1902   London.

Michel, Genevieve
1989   *The Rulers of Tikal.* Publications Vista, Guatemala,
        Central America.

Miller, Arthur G.
1973   *The Mural Painting of Teotihuacán.* Dumbarton
        Oaks, Washington, D.C.

Miller, Mary Ellen
1986   *The Art of Mesoamerica from Olmec to Aztec.*
        Thames and Hudson, London.

Millon, Rene
1973   *Urbanization at Teotihuacán, Mexico.* 2 vols. Uni-
        versity of Texas Press, Austin.

1981   "Teotihuacán: City, State, and Civilization." In *Sup-
        plement to the Handbook of Middle American In-
        dians.* Vol. 1: *Archaeology.* Edited by Victoria R.
        Bricker and Jeremy A. Sabloff. University of Texas
        Press, Austin.

Morley, Sylvanus
1983   *The Ancient Maya.* 4th ed. Stanford University
        Press, Stanford.

Pendergast, David M.
1976   *Altún Ha: A Guidebook to the Ancient Maya Ruins.*
        2d ed. University of Toronto Press, Toronto.

Prescott, William H.
1859   *History of the Conquest of Mexico.* Modern Li-
        brary, New York.

Proskouriakoff, Tatiana
1950   *A Study of Classic Maya Sculpture.* Carnegie Inst.
        Publ. 593, Washington, D.C.
1976   *An Album of Maya Architecture.* University of
        Oklahoma Press, Norman.

Reeinos, Adrian, and Delia Goetz
1953   *The Annals of the Cakchiquels.* University of
        Oklahoma Press, Norman.

Robertson, Merle Greene
1983   *The Sculpture of Palenque.* 3 vols. Princeton Univer-
        sity Press, Princeton, N.J.

Roys, Ralph
1967   *The Book of the Chilam Balam of Chumayel.* Uni-
        versity of Oklahoma Press, Norman.

Sabloff, Jeremy A.
1985   *Late Lowland Maya Civilization: Classic to Post-
        Classic.* School of American Research, University of
        New Mexico Press, Albuquerque.

Sanders, William T., and Barbara Price
1968   *Mesoamerica.* Random House, New York.

Schele, Linda, and Mary Miller
1986   *The Blood of Kings, Dynasty and Ritual in Maya
        Art.* Kimbell Art Museum, Fort Worth, Tex.

Spores, Ronald
1967   *The Mixtec Kings and Their People.* University of
        Oklahoma Press, Norman.

Stephens, John Lloyd
1841   *Incidents of Travel in Central America, Chiapas and
        Yucatán.* 2 vols. Harper, New York, Reprinted by
        Dover, 1962.
1843   *Incidents of Travel in Yucatán.* 2 vols. Harper, New
        York. Reprinted by Dover, 1963.

Stirling, Matthew
1968   "Early History of the Olmec Problem." In *Dumbar-
        ton Oaks Conference on the Olmec, 1967.* Dumbar-
        ton Oaks Research Library and Collection, Trustees
        for Harvard University, Washington, D.C.

Stuart, Gene S.

1988   *America's Ancient Cities*. National Geographic Society, Washington, D.C.

Stuart, George E.

1989   "City of Kings and Commoners, Copán." *National Geographic* Vol. 176, No. 4, October 1989, 488–504.

Tozzer, Alfred M.

1941   *Landa's Relacion de las Cosas de Yucatán.* Papers of the Peabody Museum of American Archaeology and Ethnology, vol. 18. Harvard University, Cambridge.

Wauchope, Robert (ed)

1964–   *Handbook of Middle American Indians.* (a multi-
1976   volume series) University of Texas Press, Austin.

Weaver, Muriel Porter

1981   *The Aztecs, Maya, and Their Predecessors.* 2d ed. Seminar Press, New York.

Willey, Gordon R.

1966   *An Introduction to American Archaeology*, vol. 1: *North and Middle America.* Prentice-Hall, Englewood Cliffs, N.J.

Willey, Gordon R., and Jeremy A. Sabloff

1974   *A History of American Archaeology.* Freeman, San Francisco.

1988   *Tabasco: Comalcalco.* Gobierno del Estado de Tabasco. SEFICOT. Direction de Turismo.

Acknowledgments

We are grateful to the governments of Mexico, Guatemala, Belize, and Honduras for allowing us to fly through their airspace and to photograph these magnificent Mesoamerican ruins from the air and ground.

Our special thanks go to R.E.W. Adams who read the text and captions, offered invaluable suggestions concerning the book's form and content, and wrote the Foreword; to Carolyn Tate for assistance in interpreting iconography; to Linda Schele for furnishing us with much information on the Maya; and to Michael D. Coe for his continuing encouragement.

Thanks as well go to Ethne Barnes for the schematic drawings, which assist identification of specific buildings in many aerial photographs, and to L. A. Villarreal who acted as cataloger for the thousands of photographs and negatives.

Index